Flame-out

Flame-out

From Prosecuting Jeffrey MacDonald
to Serving Time to Serving Tables

James Blackburn

L E S L I E   B O O K S ,   L . P .

Teresa,
    Very nice to meet
you!
    Your team is
better than mine!
        Jim
1/30/06

For Marsha, Jeff, and Stacy

LIBRARY OF CONGRESS CATALOGING-IN-PUBLICATION DATA

Blackburn, James L.
   Flame-out: From Prosecuting Jeffrey MacDonald to
Serving Time to Serving Tables
   1.   cm.
Includes bibliographic essay
Library of Congress Card Number: 00-190025
ISBN 0-9677374-0-0

Book Design by Kachergis Book Design, Inc.

Photographs on pages iii, 13, 25, 39, 49, 57, 107, 121, 185 and the cover courtesy of The Raleigh News & Observer.

Contents

Illustrations

Foreword

This is an important book written by a man who has something to say about climbing to the top of a mountain and then,having surveyed the summit and planted a flag, suddenly feels the entire mountain explode beneath him into dust and rubble. Few have climbed as high as Jim Blackburn and even fewer have endured the stomach-flopping experience of a complete descent in a single moment.

Jim Blackburn was a superb prosecutor. He was a splendid lawyer. He was the last person I would have expected to be in trouble. Everyone loved Jim. He was a great friend despite the fact that we had clashed frequently over cases he prosecuted. We learned that we had enough in common to build a rich friendship. I admired him and enjoyed his company immeasurably.

Jim had few equals as a prosecutor because he was so unfailingly courteous to defendants and their lawyers that jurors loved him and wanted to take him home with them, just to stay a few weeks and visit, make coffee, play checkers, and maybe fish a little. It was impossible to "out nice" Mr. Blackburn. His successes were celebrated and quite public.

Some people say that the Jeffrey MacDonald case has a supernatural power which draws people into a maelstrom and destroys them if they too fully embrace it. I have never believed that about it. I simply believe that Jeffrey MacDonald is not guilty and that his struggle to achieve a new trial is itself a courageous and remarkable evidence of his innocence. However, in winning a jury verdict in the Jeffrey MacDonald case, Jim Blackburn breathed rarified air which, regardless of whether it was supernatural, it was, nevertheless both intoxicating and dangerous. He came to be identified almost entirely with that case and after his days as a prosecutor were ended his clients expected the same spectacular success. This he could not deliver. Like a matador who reaches the pinnacle of success and disappoints the crowds so that ultimately, taking even greater risks, he is killed by the bull, Mr. Blackburn could not deliver and, because by this time he had sunk into deep and profound depression, he took greater and greater risks so that one day he started to make up the victories he could not attain otherwise. This he forthrightly acknowledges in the book.

Indeed the Jeffrey MacDonald case occupies many pages of this book. Even now Mr. Blackburn is unable to escape the case, and like a black hole it tugs at him, inviting him to oblivion. My disagreement with Jim Blackburn about the facts of the Mac-Donald case are well known, and I will not comment further except to say that with his rendition of the facts and conclusions I most emphatically disagree. He is well aware of this disagreement, which is now twenty years old. I resist further comment for fear that I shall reveal, in a moment of weakness, my own obsession with the case. My brother says that when we were boys I pinned him in a boyhood tussle and struck him, all the while shouting that he should control his temper. Both Mr. Blackburn and I are at risk of becoming caricatures of ourselves and of our views in the ancient and important matter of MacDonald.

The most important features of this story are the revelations through these pages of the courage to accept the truth about depression and to humbly and forthrightly work to overcome it. In his struggles Jim Blackburn had the benefit of Dr. Jean Spaulding, without whose excellent medical care he could not have endured the months and even years of living with depression and dealing with it. He had the love and devotion of his family. He had the excellent care of his attorney Richard Gammon, with whom I joined in a most satisfying association.

All the king's horses and all the king's men and women could not have put Jim Blackburn back together again, however, had he not been made of very remarkable stuff. Indeed, I have never seen such courage in the face of darkness. Time and again, when anyone else would have fallen into a pit of despair, he would smile and take it. At the end he told the whole world the truth about himself and of his deeds, saying, in effect, that justice should roll down like a mighty river. Once he told the whole truth about himself, he was freer than any of his detractors.

Within these pages is hope for people who are battling depression or whose loved ones battle it. Jim Blackburn became Job, sitting beside the road, covered in ashes and dust. He looked in a mirror and saw the truth and then, fearlessly, he spoke it. He worked as a waiter. He laughed at himself. He never gave up.

As I write this foreword, Jim continues his journey. I wish for him and his family the peace of the running waves and the gentle winds.

WADE M. SMITH
November 1999

Thank You

Judge Franklin Dupree used to say that you shouldn't try to name all the people you need to thank or recognize because inevitably you would leave someone out. They knew who they were anyway.

But a number of people made the trip to hell and back with me that common decency requires that I mention. First, my family. The very first day I told Marsha about everything going wrong, she asked me what I wanted her to do. I said I wanted her to stay but that she was free to do whatever she wanted. I knew she hadn't bargained for this. She responded, "They said for better or worse. We've had better. I guess this is the time for worse." It doesn't get much better than that. Though her humor has flagged at times, her support has never wavered.

Jeff and Stacy—they are the two strongest people I know. They and Marsha gave, and continue to give, the best meaning of unconditional love. When I told Stacy I was writing this "Thank You," she said she expected me to write that she was the most wonderful daughter in the world and that Jeff was the greatest son in the world. So, there, I have said it.

I had an incredible support group. Wade Smith and I used to tell each other that if one of us got in trouble, each would immediately use the other for help. Of course, neither of us ever thought the other would be in trouble. But I was. So I called him, he was there, and he has always remained so. I am particularly grateful to Wade for graciously agreeing to write the foreword for this book.

I was the first person to tell Rick Gammon that he had passed the state bar exam. I am truly thankful he did, for he is one of the best lawyers I know anywhere. I am very lucky to have him on my side.

The third musketeer was Dr. Jean Spaulding, who I wish I had never had to meet under professional circumstances. She is the world's greatest psychiatrist. I am grateful she had a cancellation that first day so I could see her.

Before I go further, let me say that without these six people, individually or as a group, I would not be here today telling you this story. They gave me the lifeline I needed, and they never let go.

My two brothers, Glenn and Bill, never wavered, not once, in their love and support for me. Glenn visited me in the hospital at Duke University Medical Center, and often in Raleigh, and Bill tried his best to get in uninvited into a medium-security prison one Saturday afternoon in the dead of winter. My mother is wonderful. She thought everything was someone else's fault; she was with me completely. So was my father. He passed away a little more than a year ago, and his last words to me were, "Do you still make a $100 a night at that restaurant, and do you think you will ever get your law license back?" Family is good.

Senator Robert Morgan gave me my first job when I was twenty-five years old, a baby lawyer, and he was the state's newly elected attorney general. Talk about unconditional friendship. He gave me a job on work release in his law office, took me public places when I was afraid to go by myself, and was the first and last to defend me to anyone.

Two favorite friends are Sheila Singleton and Charlie Hinton. I used to kid Sheila that the reason she smiled so much was that she took too much medicine for depression. But she did smile around me. For more than a year, she and Charlie picked me up when I was down and walked with me when I needed company.

Charlie even gave me college basketball tickets so that I could see my Deacons lose to his Tar Heels.

Melany McFall and Alison Rousseau worked for my old law firm. During the worst year of my life, they took me to lunch, cooked dinner for me, and, most importantly of all, just listened.

Joe McGinniss, author of *Fatal Vision,* a book about Jeffrey MacDonald, lives in Massachusetts, but in 1993 he seemed as close as right next door. He was a phone call away, and he frequently checked on me to make sure I was doing well. He sent me books to read in the hospital and wrote letters to cheer me up. The only time I have won anything was on Kentucky Derby Day that year when he won ten dollars for me on a long-shot bet on the winning horse.

To George Sloan for picking me up every day at prison and taking me to work release, to Frank Colvard for being my friend and encouraging me to write this story, to Brent James for all his ideas about writing about Jeffrey MacDonald and this story, to Shelia Jones for reading this manuscript and trying to think of a title, to Stephanie Gibbs for initially editing my work and hoping she hadn't made me too angry by doing so, thank you.

To everyone at Kachergis Book Design, particularly Anne Theilgard and her mother Joyce Kachergis, and to Judy Davis for her careful suggestions and editing, a special thank you. Encouragement is a wonderful thing, and all of you gave it in abundance.

I first met Pat Boyce when she was the campus beauty queen at Wake Forest University, and I was a small campus faculty brat. She and her lawyer husband, Gene Boyce, were two of the first to read this manuscript and think it worthwhile. They gave me the confidence that I should write about what happened to me.

Finally, the southern belle, Mary Mac Pope, who used to be a trial court judge in North Carolina and now practices law. What she really does is drive beautiful cars, cook delicious dinners, and encourage ex-lawyers to make something of themselves and write. Without her, there would be no book.

To all of these people and those whom I have not named, but fall under the Dupree rule, who were and are there for me, I can only say thank you and, "Until we meet again, may God hold you in the palm of His hand."

Starting Over

Have you ever had to start over? I have. It happened a few years ago, in 1993, when I was a practicing attorney with one of the biggest and most successful law firms in North Carolina. For many years, I enjoyed a wonderful reputation as a caring lawyer, truthful to judges and other lawyers, a good and competent trial lawyer, and a former federal prosecutor who had been the lead attorney in the triple murder conviction of Green Beret Dr. Jeffrey MacDonald in 1979.

For a time I was golden. In the words of one local state prosecutor, I was everyone's hero, the one who did good and won the biggest criminal case of a lifetime. Before I prosecuted Dr. Mac-Donald, I had never seen a murder trial, much less been involved in one. That was no problem. Neither had my co-counsel or the presiding judge. This was federal court, and we didn't do murder cases.

Until 1979. Dr. Jeffrey MacDonald is the only person I ever prosecuted who was truly presumed innocent at the beginning of the trial. He had the best lawyers, top-notch expert witnesses, and, of course, if things got tight he could always testify himself and blow both the jury and me away.

I guess that was the strategy. The only thing is it didn't work. He lost. We won. He went to prison for three life terms. He was briefly released about a year later when an appellate court said he hadn't received a speedy trial, but the U.S. Supreme Court sent him back to prison on a six to three vote. He has been there ever since.

I went to prison myself on January 3, 1994, for a period of three and one-half months, following a plea of guilty to multiple felony counts of wrongdoing that included forgery, embezzlement, and obstruction of justice. Before I was indicted, I voluntarily turned in my license to practice law. I was formally disbarred several weeks later. Thus, for a short period of time, both Jeffrey MacDonald and I were behind bars.

Fortunately for me, I was released on April 26, 1994. The world is very different for someone who has just been released from prison, has no job, and may no longer practice the only profession he has known. It isn't like plumbing. You can't just start doing it again.

Also, I was pretty angry with everyone, including myself. I thought, "What the hell do I do now? I don't know how to do anything but be a lawyer."

Earlier, I was diagnosed by two psychiatrists as bordering on manic depression, suffered a walking-around nervous breakdown with psychotic features, and I'd had a break with reality. On top of that, I was told I had a crippling personality disorder in that I sought too much to please. I was simply much too nice to everyone I met. I couldn't tell anyone no.

So, I had to start over. How? And doing what?

My recovery started with going back to the basics that we learn while growing up. None of them were new. They were all rather simple, really. They were just very difficult for me to do, particularly when I hadn't been doing them for some time. Now, maybe none of these principles apply to you. You may be perfect. Or lucky. You may never have to start anything over. But if you do, and you are not perfect, then these next few points may mean something to you. They certainly did to me.

After a few years of working my way back from disaster, I realized that I had to adopt certain traits and follow certain guidelines to make any progress. Worse, I couldn't pick and choose, I had to use them all. And I had to do better at this than I had ever done anything in my life, including prosecuting MacDonald.

Here they are, in no particular order except for the first one, which always has to remain first.

Have faith in God and face your fears
Humility
Anger is good
Laughing is better
Always do your best
Give and accept love—unconditionally
Learn what makes you happy and do it
Learn to forgive yourself and others
Always go the second or even third mile
Never . . . ever . . . give up
Believe . . . always believe . . . in angels

I didn't find these principles in a book or on a card or printed anywhere. I just learned them. They are true. They are real. And there are no shortcuts.

When I tried cases and lost, I always felt sorry for myself. But I learned from a wise federal judge who told me if I ever hoped to be any good, I had to get myself together and try the next case . . . and the next case . . . and so on, until I won.

The same is true of these principles. Because you fail on one or more doesn't mean you give up. Never do that. You pick yourself up and start again. And one day, you'll recover.

I wish it was easy to start over. It is not. It is one of the most difficult challenges we humans face. We have to change the way we were. With no guarantee of success.

At a low point in my life—while I was in prison at Troy, North Carolina—I received a visit from two close friends, Sheila Singleton and Charlie Hinton. They'd driven from Raleigh to see me and let me know they loved me. I awaited them on my side of the visiting room. I was dressed in a brown prisoner's uniform. They came in and smiled. I did the same. I was in handcuffs and a glass partition separated us.

Sheila was in her early forties, with short dark hair and a perpetual smile. I had known her about a year, meeting her after she read in the newspaper that I'd just been in Duke Hospital suffering, in part, from depression. At that time, we met for coffee early one morning and talked about the problems of mental illness and, in particular, depression.

Sheila suffered from depression, and it had robbed her of years of her life. We developed instant empathy, and for all that year she was one of my strongest, most supportive friends. If I needed a ride, she took me. If I was down, she cheered me up. She attended every court hearing, took part in every major decision that affected my life, and was at my home the night I was sentenced to prison. It was no surprise to me that she and Charlie drove from Raleigh to a prison in the middle of the state to see me.

And Charlie. He was a real estate lawyer in town. From the beginning, when my troubles were first publicized, he was there for me. We walked everywhere together, often in the early mornings when it was biting cold. We once got lost in William B. Umstead State Park, a local park not fifteen minutes from Raleigh. We started walking early one morning on a well-known hiking trail and then, totally lost in conversation, became totally lost in the woods. By the time we found our way out, it was almost lunchtime. Like Sheila, he felt he needed to come see me.

We exchanged hellos. Shelia smiled and asked how I was. I raised my hands to let them see the handcuffs. She looked down, then right back at me, and very quietly told me that she and Charlie had bad news to tell me.

"Bad news? What do you mean bad news? What do you think this is?"

"No, Jim, something much worse has happened. It's about Pete Carruthers. He's been diagnosed with an inoperable brain tumor. He's not going to live. Nothing can be done for him."

Pete was a Presbyterian minister and one of my best friends. He was short, had very dark hair and a mustache that made him proud. He was the only male in a family of five. I saw Pete just two days before I went to prison. He'd had a seizure several days before and was lying quietly on the floor in front of a crackling fire in a raised fireplace. He hadn't known yet what was wrong with him, but he was hopeful that it was not serious.

Pete had been with me the day before I was indicted by a grand jury. He had visited with me at Duke Hospital. We had walked in the woods together with his black Lab and talked of the future. He was very young. Now he'd received a death sentence.

Before he died, Pete had one more wonderful gift for me and all who heard him preach one day at his church in Raleigh. It came in the words of an Easter sermon, not long before he died. This is some of what he said that day:

> . . . The beginning of Passion Week, when suffering takes on such reality that we know there is no short cut around Good Friday. There is no quick and easy Easter. The sacrifice acceptable to God is not what the world would tell us, as in "The five traits of highly successful people." No, the sacrifice acceptable to God is a broken spirit; and a broken and contrite heart. Highly effective people in this life don't ordinarily show their success by way of their brokenness. . . . But God chooses to work through wounded, broken persons—and the wounded and broken learn to be honest with their brokenness. Life is raw, life is real, life is full of "lumps in our throats" and fears that keep us up alone in the dark night. Remind us, Holy God, that while our prayers may not be granted as they are prayed, they are heard. When Your will crosses our own inclinations, help us in our brokenness to be led like children; so strengthen our faith. Help us with courage, to look at our own failure and brokenness—to offer it to You to transform it to power for care and service.

In the weeks before Pete died, he invited everyone he knew to sit in the front pews with his family at the funeral. On the day of his memorial service, the church filled with people who had been told they were his best friends. So, the minister declared the whole church to be the front pews.

I remembered Pete's Easter sermon that day. His words weren't spoken or written to sell a best-selling book. They didn't promise great material riches. They didn't guarantee that you would get ahead in your professional career if you followed them. They just told you of the sacrifice that is acceptable to God.

I did not want to become a broken person, but I did. In almost every way. In the years that followed, I have thought a lot about what it takes to overcome deep adversity. For me, it took a complete faith in God and the best of friends. It was not smooth going. Sometimes I felt and acted as if I were alone. I wasn't.

It has been hard for me to accept Pete's words. I believe it is difficult to accept God's will rather than your own. It is much easier to read a self-help book that tells you how to think positively, act aggressively, and get ahead.

This story doesn't promise any of that. It is rather a story of someone who rose very high, fell very low, and tried to figure out what the hell went wrong, and how to become once again a man his children would admire. This is my story. I am trying to be like Pete.

Death of a Family

In Fayetteville, North Carolina, on February 17, 1970, the last person Kristen ever saw was her father. The last person who ever held her was her father. The last person she ever spoke to was her father. It was three days after Valentine's Day. She had given him a card that told him he was the greatest daddy in the world. Kristen gave up fighting and everything went black.

He took her little two-year-old body and, after knowing she was dead and beyond pain, stabbed her over and over again as she lay in his lap, first with the ice pick and then with the knife. He placed her back in her bed and pulled the covers up around her. Her soft blonde hair lay across her cheek as the bottle with a residue of chocolate milk was put near her mouth. As though she had nodded off to sleep, still sucking out the last drops of nourishment.

He might have looked at her one last time before striding quickly out of the room to the master bedroom just steps away. In the middle of this room was Colette, his wife, now five months pregnant, lying on her back, with her blood-stained pink pajamas pushed up around her legs, eyes gazing upward but unknowing. Walking to her, he took the ice pick he'd just used on his youngest daughter Kristen and, kneeling down beside her, rammed it into Colette's body at least twenty-four times. Twenty-one of those stabs went in her chest. In his delirium, he did not notice that his torn blue pajama top was stretched out across her chest, with a sleeve draping onto the floor.

Finally, he checked on his oldest daughter Kimberly, whose bedroom was across the hall from Kristen's. Looking in at her from the doorway, he saw her lying in her bed with the covers pulled up around her, the left side of her pretty face on the pillow and her long blonde hair trussed up around her. She was very still.

Satisfied that all was done, he crossed the hall yet again to the closet near the bathroom and pulled out of the cabinet the scalpel that he needed. Taking two steps into the bathroom and turning on the light, he looked in the mirror above the sink and, taking a deep breath, inserted the scalpel into the right side of his chest. Such an insertion can be used as a treatment called pneumothorax, a therapeutic measure induced to collapse a lung. Blood spurted from the wound into the sink in front of him, but he was too dazed to notice.

He could barely make it to the telephone in the kitchen where he placed a 911 call for help, telling the operator that people were getting killed and they needed medics at 544 Castle Drive as soon as possible.

Having enough breath to make it to the cabinet under the kitchen sink, he opened the door and pulled out a latex surgical glove. Putting it on his right hand, he walked to the master bedroom and stuck his fingers repeatedly in his dead wife's blood and scrawled the word "PIG" on the headboard of their bed. He tore the glove off into pieces and called the operator one more time to find out what was taking so long to get medical help to his family.

He dropped down beside his wife and rested, still hurting from his self-inflicted wound and the emotional trauma that he felt from just having murdered his entire family.

This was not, of course, the story that Jeffrey MacDonald told. In fact, it would be more than nine years before this story would be told in public to a federal jury sitting in judgment of him at his criminal trial in the summer of 1979 in Raleigh, North Carolina. By that time, Jeffrey MacDonald had told his story of innocence thousands of times. He knew it well. His story differed widely from this one.

He was baby-sitting the children that night while his wife was away at Fayetteville Technical Community College, taking a psychology class. He washed the dishes, put the children to bed, and waited for her to come home. They had a mixed drink and talked about their new baby. They hoped it would be a boy. Colette was tired and slowly walked down the hallway to go to sleep.

He was restless and stayed up to watch a little of Johnny Carson's "Tonight Show." After the show, he fell asleep on the living room sofa, while reading the Mickey Spillane book, *Kiss Me Deadly*. Everything was quiet and peaceful.

Sometime in the early morning hours, he awakened to the cries of his oldest daughter Kimberly, crying, "Daddy, Daddy, Daddy, Daddy," and Colette's scream, "Jeff, Jeff, Jeff, why are they doing this to me?"

Just as he started up to help, he was knocked down on the couch by a black man carrying a club that resembled a baseball bat. Two other men thrust an ice pick and knife at him. Out of the corner of his eye, he saw in the distance a young white woman with long blonde hair and a floppy hat, holding something that looked like "a flickering light, like a candle," all the while chanting, "Acid is groovy. Kill the pigs."

He struggled with the intruders, but he was no match for the three of them. He recalled his blue pajama top being torn and pulled over his head and around his wrists. Then he fell unconscious at the step leading to the hallway to the bedrooms.

Waking up to a deathly quiet, he walked quickly to his bedroom where Colette lay on her back. He tore off his pajama top, he said, and placed it on her chest to keep her warm. Seeing a knife protruding from her chest, he pulled it out and threw it to the floor near the dresser.

He walked to his kids' rooms and took their pulses. He got

none. He went back to Colette and tried to resuscitate her. He could not. They were all dead. Only he was alive. He called for help . . . twice . . . they were so slow in coming. He hurt so much from his own wounds. By his count, he had almost eighteen to twenty life-threatening wounds, mainly from the ice pick. He had been struck by the club at least six times. He could barely stay conscious.

So, he collapsed on the floor beside his wife, with his two little girls in nearby rooms, and passed out. His last thoughts were of the farm in Connecticut that he and Colette were going to buy, and the family they were going to raise, and the dogs and ponies they would have.

Joining the MacDonald Case

I can barely remember a time in my adulthood when Jeffrey MacDonald and the crimes he committed were not a part of my life. This case changed my perception of who I am and what I should be able to accomplish. As of this writing, it has been twenty years since the summer of 1979 when the United States Government, with myself as the lead prosecutor, convicted the former Green Beret Army captain and doctor of killing his pregnant wife Colette, his five-year-old daughter Kimberly, and his two-year-old daughter Kristen.

Not a day has gone by since that summer that I haven't thought about that night almost thirty years ago when time stopped at 544 Castle Drive on the Fort Bragg military base in Fayetteville, North Carolina. Though the trial is long over and MacDonald's appeals to the federal appellate courts have been rejected, he still maintains his innocence, still refuses to ask for parole, and is now seeking vindication through the new DNA testing.

His main nemesis, Alfred (Freddy) Kassab, his former father-in-law, is dead, having passed away in 1994 of emphysema. Colette's mother, Mildred Kassab, also died in 1994 of cancer. Judge Franklin Dupree, the presiding judge at the trial, also died of cancer several years ago.

I am still here, though I no longer practice law. I am still asked almost daily about the case and am interviewed every time Mac-Donald files a new motion or requests another hearing concerning his case. I have found that time has not taken away my memories of that trial, and though many additional crimes have been committed since this one, the MacDonald murder case, in my mind, stands alone for brutality, selfishness, arrogance, intrigue, passion, adversity, deep and unrelenting sadness, and finally, the triumph of good over evil.

This case is about the government doing the right thing in the right way. It is about the jury reaching the correct decision in a timely manner, after giving both sides close and careful attention throughout the trial. It is about two young and inexperienced lawyers coming up against the best and, with no one seeing it coming, winning it all.

But it is also a case study in reality. I came to know Freddy and Mildred Kassab very well. I spent many evenings with them talking about the facts of the case before, during, and after the trial. The three of us remained friends until their deaths. When I ran into serious legal trouble myself in 1993, they immediately wrote me a kind letter of support and thanked me again for my efforts so long ago.

But I could never talk to either of them without experiencing such powerful sadness. It was simple. They missed Colette and their grandchildren. They didn't get to watch them grow up, go to college, get married, and have babies of their own. Mildred and Freddy never got over that.

If by some miracle Colette, Kimberly, and Kristen could have come back to life for just a short while, I believe Freddy and Mildred would gladly have voted to free Jeffrey MacDonald from prison in trade. But of course that was impossible and so, with Freddy taking the lead, they spent the rest of their lives pursuing their child's killer. Once they saw him convicted and put in prison, they stayed determined to keep him there. That was, in

Freddy and Mildred Kassab, Jeffrey MacDonald's in-laws, fought nine
years to bring MacDonald to trial

their minds, a small price to pay for what he had done to their
family and their lives.

People have told me over the years that Freddy Kassab was obsessed, and certainly Jeffrey MacDonald has thought so. But
then, who wouldn't be? His daughter and granddaughters lay in
the ground in a Long Island cemetery, their futures stolen from
them with knives, an ice pick, and a hard wooden club. The man
they believed responsible started a new life in California in medicine and with women. They could not stand for that, and they
vowed to stop him and bring him to justice. They did so.

This is also the story of two young lawyers, Brian Murtagh, a career lawyer for the United States Justice Department, and myself as Assistant United States Attorney for the Eastern District of North Carolina. Brian was from New York, where his mother was a schoolteacher. He had been assigned to the Justice Department to assist veteran prosecutor Victor Woerhide in trying MacDonald. Brian's job originally was to oversee the physical evidence and help prepare Woerhide, who would try the case.

The case was originally going to be tried in the summer of 1975. Last-minute appeals to the appellate courts won a stay of the proceedings, and the trial did not occur that year or the next. Then Victor Woerhide died of a heart attack.

By all rights, Jeffrey MacDonald should have had it won then. His trial was stopped by the Fourth Circuit Court of Appeals, which stated that his right to a speedy trial had been injured, and the only man who at that time could try his case was now dead. If ever there was a time for him to pop the champagne cork, that was it.

Time, however, was not on Jeffrey MacDonald's side; it was on Colette, Kimberly, and Kristen's side. They weren't going anywhere. They could wait for justice. By the winter of 1978, the Supreme Court of the United States heard oral argument in the Jeffrey MacDonald murder case on the issue of his denial of a speedy trial. The Supreme Court ultimately ruled against him.

During this time I joined the United States Attorney's office and met Brian Murtagh and Freddy Kassab. I have never met two men more focused on the same goal, bringing Jeffrey MacDonald to trial. Without their determination, Jeffrey MacDonald would be a free man today.

After spending a short time with them, seeing the crime scene, and reviewing portions of the grand jury testimony, I was hooked. What is unusual about this case is that so many other people felt the same way. People involved with this case were touched by it in a very personal way, and not for just a summer or the duration of the trial but for a lifetime.

It certainly affected me for a lifetime. I did not intend for that to happen. I would much prefer that at the end of 1979, the case would have been over for me, too. I thought that it was. I did stay involved in some of the early appeals. Later I worked as an informal consultant as more appeals were filed on MacDonald's behalf. Even as my involvement lessened, however, I never lost interest in the outcome of the case. I believe MacDonald is guilty and is precisely where he deserves to be.

The MacDonald case has stayed with me. Once I became involved with it, I couldn't let go. This became more than just a murder case that happened years ago. It was more than a case of vengeance by grief-stricken parents. It was not a case of government abuse and wrongdoing, as MacDonald has loudly claimed for years. This case was black and white; there were no shades of gray. Colette and her girls weren't just a little bit dead. And MacDonald wasn't just a little bit a murderer.

Colette, Kimberly, and Kristen had to wait over nine years to see their killer brought to trial, found guilty, and sent to prison for life. But that is not the worst. The worst thing, for which there is no good explanation, is that their killer was Colette's husband and Kimberly and Kristen's father.

The following pages contain some recollections of the spring and summer of 1979 and how we sent Jeffrey MacDonald to prison.

Guilty As Sin

As Brian Murtagh and I drove sixty miles from the Federal Office Building on New Bern Avenue in downtown Raleigh to Fort Bragg, located in Fayetteville, North Carolina, I steeled myself for what was coming. Almost a decade had passed since the MacDonald family was murdered, yet the Army had retained control of the apartment, had not rented it out, and indeed had kept it sealed all these years. This included keeping the electricity on and defrosting the refrigerator. I did not know what we would find.

The MacDonald apartment windows had long been boarded up to protect the privacy and security of the apartment. The outside looked barren to me, only a little shubbery around the apartment, and it was obvious no one had lived there for some time. The front door was padlocked several times, and it took us a few minutes just to open the door.

Finally it shuddered and moved. I walked inside, took a deep breath, and looked around. Little furniture remained in the living room. There was the sofa on which, according to Jeffrey MacDonald, he'd gone to sleep and been awakened early that February morning by intruders bent on killing him and his family. Nearby was the wooden coffee table that was in all the pictures, and which the Army had said had been placed on its side. A small wooden desk was just to the left of the open door, on which rested a woman's wallet, with Colette's driver's license and credit cards inside. Her brown weejuns were sitting neatly on the floor beside it.

The walls were bare, gray, and dirty. Fingerprint powder still remained after all these years. The kitchen was just off the L-shaped living and dining room. The dishes were still in the sink drain, cooking items in the cabinets, the refrigerator was still running and still stocked with food-a can of cranberry sauce and another of ginger ale. The freezer compartment had been defrosted whenever necessary over the years, and it still contained a partially used bag of french fries, a carton of chocolate ripple ice cream and another of strawberry, a box of frozen rainbow trout, and a cellophane package of freezer-burned pork chops. Most poignantly, a wall calendar with the month and year was still set on February, 1970. Valentine cards from Kimberly and Kristen, addressed to the "greatest daddy in the world," were on the counter.

Walking to the main hallway, I noticed a pair of very small blue tennis shoes on the floor. The bedroom to the right had been Kimberly's. Some games were still there, as were a paper drawing and a clown. Kristen's room across the hall was less full, but the frame of her small bed was clearly visible.

Then there was the room at the end of the hall where it all started. Where Colette fought for her life and the lives of her children and lost. Where her arms had been broken, her skull cracked, and her body stabbed with an ice pick and paring knife over and over again. Where she had the stare of death as she lay there in the early morning hours of February 17, 1970. Her clothes were still on the chair beside the bed. Large chunks of the carpet where she had bled so profusely from her head had been cut out and removed. If you looked closely, you could see the word "PIG" written in Type A blood—Colette's blood type—still on the headboard.

I stayed there for a few minutes and just stared. Neither Brian nor I spoke. I went to the remaining rooms, the hall bathroom, the utility room just off the master bedroom, and the bathroom next to it.

The apartment wasn't gruesome so much as depressing. Such an absence of life there. It was not a place where you lingered for long. You wanted to see it and leave.

Slowly over the months that followed, seeing that apartment, studying the photographs of that night, reviewing the notes, depositions, and testimony of dozens of witnesses, including MacDonald, I felt like Freddy and Brian. I became passionate.

This case demanded passion. If you weren't willing to commit your very being to the prosecution of this case, you didn't belong on the case. One of the good things about being an inexperienced trial lawyer is that you don't know what you don't know. We didn't know the odds we were up against. We didn't know how much smarter and more sophisticated the other side's lawyers were. We didn't know that everyone thought we were hopelessly outmatched and couldn't possibly win a conviction. We didn't know how much the case would consume us.

We only knew that we thought MacDonald was guilty of killing his family and that we had overwhelming evidence on our side. My family, Marsha and Jeff, then just four years old, became tightly involved as well. When I sat in the backyard dictating notes, Jeff sat beside me on the ground and pretended to dictate notes as well.

Almost every night, Marsha and I sat around the dining room table and discussed the many statements MacDonald made over the years and how I should cross-examine him. We tried to think of every way possible that he could not be responsible for the deaths of his family. We never thought of a single one.

The evidence had not been looked at in years. It was stored at FBI Headquarters in Washington, D.C. Brian and I spent a week there during March, reviewing the evidence and talking to the many agents who would later testify.

We had no idea whether any of the potential witnesses were still alive, and if so, where they were.

The pictures of the MacDonald apartment were not in any kind of order. We didn't even know what constituted a complete set of the pictures for the case. They were scattered throughout several boxes.

No one thought the case would ever go to trial. Probably everyone alive with any experience and good sense took one look at it and ran the other way. A lot of people thought MacDonald was guilty of murder, but almost no one believed a jury would convict him.

I remember reading a letter that a previous United States attorney had written to the Justice Department. It stated that he believed MacDonald was guilty of murdering his family, that the evidence supported it, but that his own personal time could not be spent on the case because he had to train his new Assistant United States Attorneys. And so, would the Justice Department please handle the matter?

I took entire files home with me at night, one at a time. I would sit up until the early morning hours every night for months reading and then dictating outlines of previous testimony of every person who said anything to anyone about the Mac-Donald case.

We found that all of our witnesses were still alive and willing to testify. We could refresh their memories by allowing them to review their previous testimony from the military hearing that had taken place in 1970. We learned that most of them could not forget this case. They had become like us.

I remember interviewing the two pathologists who examined the two children. Each doctor was very clinical when discussing his own patient and notes. But when it came to the other child, each doctor became emotional. Their professional demeanor faded and they reacted personally. Each was intensely affected by what he saw and read.

I learned that people were appalled by the horrific nature of this crime. The time span, which had gone from February 1970 to the beginning of the trial in July 1979, could be wiped away in seconds just by showing the jury the photographs. It might as well have happened yesterday.

The idea of focus groups had not yet taken hold in American legal proceedings, so I invented my own. I would share some of what I knew about the case with trusted friends, looking at their reactions and seeing what took hold. I wanted to know how important it was to destroy MacDonald's character, how significant it was that we didn't really know his motive.

What about all his girlfriends? Did people care? Did they have anything to do with the murders? What if these girls still liked him?

Was he a good doctor? Did that make any difference? If he saved a bunch of people today, did that make up for killing one yesterday? Did God keep score?

What about the hippies? Did they exist in reality, or just in MacDonald's mind? Had he seen some hippies previously and pulled from that experience his descriptions of the hippies that night to lend credibility to his story?

How important were his different stories and lies about his physical injuries? Why did he keep changing the number of wounds he received? Did anybody care? Why did he lie about things he didn't have to, such as the presence of an ice pick in the house on top of the refrigerator? Why did he argue the club did not come from the house, even after paint samples and wood grain proved that it did? Why didn't he just keep his mouth shut?

We had so many questions that spring, but Brian and I soon decided on what turned out to be the correct trial strategy. We would try our case, not theirs. They would get their chance. But if we lost, we would do so knowing that every good argument the government had developed over the years would be put before the jury. We would make them play on our side of the court.

Our first two witnesses were members of the military police (MP). They were only two of ten that we could have called. We wanted to show the immediate condition of the MacDonald apartment, as it was when help first arrived. Sergeant Richard S.

Tevere was the first one inside the apartment. Tevere was a heavy-set young man from New York City, who in 1970 was living in the South for the first time.

The back door was open. He and others walked inside, through the utility room and to the bedroom, where they saw Colette lying on her back with Jeffrey MacDonald lying next to her. MacDonald made a noise, and it was clear he was still alive. The MPs asked him who had done this to him, and he started telling the story of the hippie intruders.

Then he asked about his kids. The MPs looked at each other. They hadn't been aware of any children. Slowly they went down the hallway and looked into the two bedrooms, shining their flashlights at the two beds. They were the first outsiders to see the bodies of Kimberly and Kristen.

The first crime scene photographer had to be replaced after he got sick looking at the bodies. The second one came, and before anyone was moved, shot the picture record. We used some of those pictures in 1979 at the murder trial.

Soon, Agents Bill Ivory and Bob Shaw of the Army Criminal Investigative Division (CID) arrived. Ivory was the lead investigator, a careful man with a sharp eye and a keen wit. Bob Shaw was quiet, methodical, and always under control at any crime scene. Together, they sealed off the apartment. They asked a neighbor, Mr. Kalin, who lived upstairs, to come down and identify the bodies. MacDonald himself was still alive, though the extent of his injuries was not then known. He was taken immediately to the emergency room of Womack Army Hospital.

As MacDonald left the apartment on his gurney, he called back about his kids, again wanting to know how they were, and, by the way, tell the agents that he pulled a knife out of Colette's chest and threw it somewhere in the room after first wiping it off.

All of these initial factors would later play a large part in our trial strategy.

"Brian, why do you suppose MacDonald kept asking about his kids when he obviously knew they were dead?"

"Probably two reasons, Jim. First, he wanted to make sure they were dead. I mean, the last thing he needed now was for someone to survive. Second, it's a red herring, to throw everyone off. Fake his concern."

"What about the knife?"

"You know, that's strange. Almost anyone will tell you that in a stabbing case, you should leave the knife in the victim so as to keep the hole plugged, until you get medical treatment. Here, he says he pulled it out of her chest and threw it away."

"Why do you think he said that?"

"The knife found on the floor beside the dresser is the one that he says he pulled out of her chest, the Geneva Forge knife. But it's dull, not like the paring knife. And Paul Stombaugh, the Federal Bureau of Investigation Laboratory expert thinks the Geneva Forge knife was used to make the cuts in the arm sleeve of MacDonald's pajama top. The hole there is consistent with that kind of knife."

"So?"

"So, that knife was never inside Colette's body. It doesn't have her blood on it. Paul thinks Colette used it to defend herself against Jeffrey during the fight in the master bedroom. He had to have an explanation as to why it was there and where it came from. So he made up the story about it being in her chest. Yet that knife is not consistent with any of the wounds in her chest."

"Brian, when we start calling the MPs, what do you think about using Kenneth Mica as a witness for us?"

"Mica, why? He's the one who says he saw a young woman at the corner of Lucas and Honeycutt, not far from the MacDonald home."

"I know, but here's the thing. We've got ten MPs. We don't want to use them all. If we do, the other side will turn this trial into a farce, showing how screwed up the crime scene was. We don't want that. We have to use Tevere because he was the first one there and his prior testimony is consistent and intelligent.

He doesn't say anything dumb. But we need one more, to give it some substance."

"But why Mica? I never have liked him."

"I know, but I've read all the MPs' transcripts. Mica is the only one to say he saw a young woman outside that night. No one else saw anybody. Now, I don't know whether he's lying or not. Or whether he just likes the fame he gets with saying something like that. But I do know that if we don't call him, they will. And then they will tell the jury we hid someone from them. If we use him ourselves, we can say, "So what?" to his testimony about the woman. We don't have to agree that it was someone who was in the *apartment* that night."

"Go on, I'm listening."

"Well, we put him on early in our case. By the time Ivory and Shaw get through, the jury will have forgotten about him. And by the time the trial's over, he's history and not a big deal. One more thing. Before it's over, I'm going to find a way to make Mica be telling the truth about seeing a woman, yet be able to tell the jury that it wasn't anyone who was at the MacDonald apartment."

"How are you going to do that?"

"Well, for starters, MacDonald has always said the young woman who was there that night had on muddy boots. Mica doesn't say anything about the woman he saw wearing boots. He says the woman he saw had "nice legs." That may be small, but it gives me something to say with a straight face."

"Let me think about it. You might be onto something."

Tevere and Mica were the first two witnesses we called at the trial. Their testimony on direct examination about the preservation of the crime scene was specific and credible. Mica testified on direct questions from me that he had seen a young woman nearby that night, but that she was not wearing boots. That statement, combined with the fact that I, the prosecuting attorney, was the one mentioning the existence of this woman, lessened the impact of her alleged presence outdoors that night.

Bernard L. Segal, MacDonald's lead defense attorney, tried his best to show the crime scene was bungled, but he only had our two witnesses with which to do it. He never called any MPs of his own. Did he think we'd put his case on for him? He was wrong. He should have been less arrogant and more prepared.

The press and even Joe McGinniss in his book about the Jeffrey MacDonald murders, *Fatal Vision,* stated that the initial stage of our presentation was off to a shaky start. Such analyses missed the point. Brian and I always believed that if our case could survive the crime scene witnesses, we had a good chance of winning. But the other side had to destroy us, not just make us shaky. Shaky for us was a win.

In 1970, 544 Castle Drive was no longer a home; it was a crime scene with three dead bodies. It was pure horror. Military officers secured the front and back doors. Evidence was carefully collected with tweezers, placed in plastic evidence bags, sealed and marked. In late March 1979, both Ivory and Shaw, the CID investigators on the scene, saw those same evidence bags again as they were slowly unsealed, the pieces of evidence pulled out, identified, introduced into evidence, and shown to the jury.

Exhibit A was a piece of ash wood, used as a club. Pieces of the club were broken off and scattered in the master bedroom. Those pieces fit back into the club, and experts testified that it was once a part of Kimberly's bed because it had identical growth rings, grain size, and composition as another piece of wood in the bed. In addition, paint from the club matched paint found on other objects in the MacDonald household. MacDonald denied ever seeing the club before, insisted that it did not come from his house, and accused the hippie intruders of having brought the club with them. These statements were false.

The club was an instrument of death. It had broken Colette's face and skull, probably both her arms, and battered Kimberly's skull as well. It was found with Type A blood on it, Colette's blood type. Traces of blood were found on the ceiling in the mas-

Center, Dr. Jeffrey MacDonald arrives at U.S. District Court in Raleigh, North Carolina, with attorneys, *left,* Wade Smith, and *right,* Bernard Segal

ter bedroom—indicating that whoever held the club swung it high enough that it sprayed blood on the ceiling.

One of the strange aspects of the case was that each member of the MacDonald family had a different blood type. Colette was Type A, Jeff was Type B, Kimberly was Type AB, and Kristen was Type O. It was therefore possible to follow the blood types around the MacDonald apartment as if they were links on a road map.

Blood drops matching Colette's Type A and also Type AB, Kimberly's type, were found on the wall of Kimberly's bedroom. Some were seven feet high. That blood got there from being sprayed by the club, probably as the club was hitting Kimberly. Her head was crushed on one side. Droplets of her blood type were found at the entrance to the master bedroom where she was probably struck the first time, which was probably when she cried the "Daddy, Daddy, Daddy, Daddy" that MacDonald quoted in his story of the events. She must have seen what was happening to her mother, and then she could cry no more. Her voice box was destroyed by the blows to the head.

Kimberly was placed in her bed, with the battered portion of her face lying against her pillow. She was tucked in. When Agent Bob Shaw found her and slowly pulled the covers back, he found underneath those covers bits of wood that matched the club and blue-black cotton threads identical to the threads in MacDonald's pajama top.

MacDonald had admitted that he checked on Kimberly to see how she was and to take her pulse. But he also always said that when he saw her the first time, he was no longer wearing his blue pajama top because he had already placed it on Colette's chest.

Bob Shaw was very careful not to disturb any evidence in Kimberly's bedroom. At the end of his direct testimony one afternoon, I asked him to come down from the witness stand and take the same sheets and bedspread and place them on a long, large table in front of the jury. Then, very slowly, very dramatically, Bob Shaw demonstrated to the jurors and the court how he removed them from the bed, saying again what he found when he did so.

The blue pajama top: This article of clothing was key to the case. MacDonald was consumed with trying to figure out how he could explain the Type A (Colette's) blood on it. So, he said he put it on Colette's chest, later further explaining that he was trying to keep her warm, and in doing so accidentally transferred some of her blood from her chest to the pajama top.

Have you ever wondered how jigsaw puzzles are made? A picture is taken, placed on the puzzle material which is then cut into all those little pieces. It remains obvious that the picture was taken before the material was cut. How else would they all fit together to show a complete picture at the end?

That same logic worked against MacDonald. The FBI concluded that the Type A blood found on MacDonald's pajama top, in at least three separate places, got there before, not after, the pajama top was torn. MacDonald testified that he was wearing it that night before the hippie intruders entered his home. He said it had no blood on it when he was wearing it earlier in the evening.

If the FBI is correct that the Type A blood got on the pajama top before and not after it was torn, how and when did it get there? Only one explanation fits. It got there when Colette was alive, bleeding from her wounds, and fighting for her life. It got there when the pajama top was torn during the struggle when MacDonald was wearing it. MacDonald's explanation was, and is, a complete ruse. The jury found that his statements on this were false.

The blue pajama top: It had forty-eight separate, perfectly round holes in it when found. MacDonald said those holes, which were not there when he was wearing it before the murder, got there because it was pulled over his head during the struggle with the hippie intruders in the living room. It became entangled in his arms, and he used it like a shield to ward off potentially lethal blows.

MacDonald had no wounds on either his arms or wrists. He had no ice pick wounds on his chest and none on his back. He had claimed between seventeen and twenty-two such life-threatening wounds in the past, but the doctors at Womack Army Hospital did not see them. All they saw were scratches and the cut in the right side of his chest that collapsed his lung.

So how did those round holes get there? The FBI concluded that if a person held the pajama top as a shield, then the force of the assailants' weapons would surely have ripped and sliced the pajama top, not made round holes. MacDonald's experts disagreed. They conducted their own experiment.

They placed a similar material on a piece of pork, tied this ham up with string, placed it on a handle, and moved the handle. Then they had a knife drop down as the ham and the material moved back and forth, back and forth. The holes in the material were round and nontearing. This proved conclusively, they said, that a knife could make round, not torn, holes in a moving object such as a pajama top.

But the night of the murders, the pajama top was not tied to a piece of ham sitting on a broomstick with a knife being lowered into it from the ceiling. According to MacDonald, it was ripped into pieces as he struggled for his life in the living room.

Shirley Green was a chemist for the FBI in the early 1970s. After carefully reviewing the photographs of twenty-one ice pick holes in Colette's chest, as well as the pictures taken earlier of the blue pajama top draped over her chest with the sleeve of the garment trailing off to her side, she took a number of probes and began putting them through the different holes in the pajama top. Over time, she discovered that she could fit twenty-one probes through forty-eight holes in the pajama top, remove the pajama top, and have made holes that matched exactly the locations of the ice pick wounds in Colette's chest.

This discovery took place years before the 1979 jury trial. No one grabbed the attention of the jurors or the concern of the defense quite as much as Shirley Green. In a sign of the times in 1979, it took a long prosecution argument with officials of the FBI to allow a woman to testify as to this important evidence. That she did so, and very well at that, was a credit to Shirley Green.

We were not through with the pajama top and its holes. Brian Murtagh cross-examined defense expert John Thornton, a bearded and balding man from California. As pre-arranged, while Brian was questioning Mr. Thornton, I went to the exhibit table and picked up the ice pick, the same one used in the murders.

Brian took a blue pajama top that he had previously bought in Washington, D. C., one that matched the original in color, white piping, and fabric. He placed it around his wrists to protect himself from me. I approached Brian and stabbed at him. I shredded the pajama top with ease and accidentally cut Brian on the wrist, stopping the trial for a moment while someone got a bandage for him.

In that simple demonstration, the lie to MacDonald's explanation was shown to the entire jury. If I had wished to really hurt or even kill Brian, I could have done so. He would have had no chance. But MacDonald, according to his story, had survived three such intruders bent on killing him. And with almost no injuries.

The blue pajama top: Two threads, soaked in Type A blood, the same as Colette's, were found on the club, which was found outside the back door of the MacDonald apartment. How did they get there? MacDonald said he never touched the club nor went outside. If the club was used against him, why didn't it have his Type B blood on it? The blue pajama top could not have been torn in the living room as MacDonald claimed, because no fibers from the pajama top were found there.

Fibers matching the blue pajama top were found in the master bedroom, however. A lot of them. More than fifty. Colette's blood was found in the master bedroom. As the club was dropped to the floor, it could easily pick up threads that had already fallen, along with Colette's blood that had already been spilled.

The blue pajama top: If MacDonald had just kept it on that night and not taken it off. When he was taken to Womack, his blue pajama bottoms were ripped off his body, thrown into the incinerator, and burned. They thought he was a stabbing *victim.*

In all likelihood, the same fate would have befallen his pajama top as well, and then no one could have found the Type A blood on the pajama top and realized it was there before the top was torn. Without the pajama top, there would have been no holes for Shirley Green to find and match up with Colette's wounds, and no control evidence with which to match up all those fibers that were found in the master bedroom and Kimberly's bed. Nor could we have matched it to the fiber found just below the headboard to Colette's and MacDonald's bed, near where someone wrote the word "PIG" in Type A blood. It was almost the perfect crime. The blue pajama top was the key to proving the case against MacDonald.

You will notice that I've barely mentioned Kristen so far. She is the most difficult victim to discuss. FBI agents who interviewed MacDonald at the hospital said he was almost indifferent when talking about either Colette or Kimberly, but he would grow pensive and silent about Kristen. Why?

In Kristen's case, MacDonald was convicted of murder in the first degree. She was blonde, blue-eyed, and two years old. She was drinking chocolate milk in her bed the night she died. The doctor who examined her discovered that her killer struck in excess of thirty times with a knife and an ice pick, plunging it over and over again into her body.

On her right hand, on one of her fingers, was a deep cut. The doctor testified at the trial that it was consistent with a defensive wound. Think about that. She fought back. She saw her killer. She knew it was her daddy. Think about that, too.

Toward the end of the trial, we kept waiting for MacDonald to come up with some new evidence and blow us out of the water. He had only two chances—Helena Stoekley and his own testimony.

MacDonald had always claimed that a young woman, with long blonde hair and wearing a floppy hat and muddy boots, was with the intruders at his home that night, that he saw her standing at the end of his sofa holding a flickering light "like a candle," saying the words, "Acid is groovy. Kill the pigs."

The year was 1970, less than one year since the Sharon Tate murders in 1969 in southern California. Indeed, a then-current issue of Esquire magazine with Lee Marvin pictured on its cover, found with blood prints on it in the MacDonald living room, also had on the cover this question: "Does Evil Lurk in California?" Inside the magazine was an article about witchcraft, which included such words as "acid" and "pigs." Did this inspire MacDonald to write "PIG" in Colette's blood?

Helena Stoeckley was a young hippie in Fayetteville during that time. She had once been a mature young girl who had babysat for officers' families at Fort Bragg. The drugs of that time had taken their toll on Helena, however, and she was not what she once was.

Helena had confessed at various times during the 1970s to being present at the MacDonald apartment the night of the killings. At other times, she denied ever being present. She made these statements to about half a dozen different people, all of whom the defense wished to call as witnesses for the defense at the MacDonald trial.

After extensive questioning outside the presence of the jury, the court ruled that Helena's prior statements were not trustworthy, because she had essentially gone both ways in her statements and because she had also been under the influence of alcohol, drugs, or both at these times. This ruling was a blow to the defense because they wanted to use these out-of-court statements to prove the truth of Helena's statements, thereby eliminating the necessity of calling Helena as a witness.

Helena was much more valuable to the defense as a testifying nonwitness than as a live witness subject to fresh cross-examination. The problem was, no one knew where she was.

The FBI found her hiding under a bed in her boyfriend's apartment in South Carolina. She was brought to Raleigh as a court witness, and both the defense and the prosecution were given a half day each to interview her in private while the trial recessed for one day.

The defense took her first on a Thursday morning. I was not happy. I was concerned that Helena would get under the spell and direction of the defense team and testify that she was indeed present at the MacDonald apartment the night of the killings, and that Jeffrey MacDonald was a victim and not the killer we had portrayed.

One of the judge's law clerks told me late that morning that it looked bad for us, that it looked as if Helena was "delivering for the defense." My heart sank.

Shortly after lunch, it was our turn. We met with her in the office of the U.S. Attorney to discuss her testimony, which would take place the next day. We did not know what she would say.

Helena sat in a dark blue chair and looked right at me. I took a deep breath and asked, "Helena, were you there that night? Did you kill anyone, or do you know anyone who did?"

"No, Mr. Blackburn, I don't. I didn't kill anyone. I have never killed anyone. I have never been to that apartment. I don't know who killed Dr. MacDonald's family."

Now, everyone in the room took a deep breath and relaxed.

The next day, Friday, shortly after lunch, it was our turn, on cross-examination, to ask Helena Stoeckley questions in front of the jury. She was just as positive then as she had been the day before. She had not been to MacDonald's apartment, had not killed anyone, did not know who had, and she had never seen Jeffrey MacDonald until that day in the courtroom.

We were very happy that weekend. They'd shot the missing-hippie-woman confession at us and missed. We had dodged a bullet that could have seriously damaged our case.

Jeffrey MacDonald had one last chance. Himself. He had previously spoken to the media, at the military court hearing, and to the grand jury. Except for the grand jury, where he told the jury they "can shove all your fucking evidence right up your ass," he had acquitted himself well. There was no reason he should think differently about the trial.

Jeffrey MacDonald has maintained for almost thirty years that he is innocent. He has also attacked anyone who disagreed with him, trying to destroy their careers in the process. He has been as brutal in that way as he was that night with his family. He shows no remorse, no concern, no empathy for anyone but himself.

As soon as the United States Army let him go in 1970, he began attacking the government agents as incompetents, liars, and fools. He said these words on national television and in national newspapers. As the investigation progressed, he attacked the government lawyers as almost evil and as people who would break any law, do any wrong, to harass him and his family.

Before the trial in 1979, and even for years thereafter, he had his lawyers attack the integrity of Brian Murtagh, attempting to get him fired from the Justice Department and ultimately disbarred.

He attacked his former in-laws, Freddy and Mildred Kassab, for being obsessed. That is where he made his worst mistake. Freddy was as determined to get Jeffrey MacDonald for the murder of his family, as Jeffrey MacDonald was determined not to get charged.

Eventually, the attacks on the government and Freddy and Mildred became too much. Eventually the government struck back, not with the illegalities that MacDonald has always claimed, but with the physical and scientific evidence that Jeffrey MacDonald left at his home that night.

MacDonald would finally, after all the weeks of what he called the government's technical and pathetic little case, have the chance to set the record straight. He'd prove to the world how much he had loved his family, how he would never hurt them in any way. Besides, he had Bernie Segal on his side, asking him the softball questions that he would knock out of the courtroom.

The other side had no one. Woerhide was dead. Murtagh was a viper, and Blackburn had no guts. Blackburn would never go after him.

I will never forget the first few minutes of MacDonald's direct testimony when Segal asked him why he had never remarried. He said, "I can't forget my wife and children." He even started to cry. He kept crying most of the day, this after going through the entire trial totally dry eyed and emotionless in front of the jury. Before he was through, even some members of the jury started to cry. I thought I'd throw up.

His testimony took the entire day. Afterwards, a spectator stopped me outside the courtroom and told me that, after that performance, I really had my work cut out for me the next day. I believed her.

Court trials are like sporting events. The momentum shifts constantly. Just when you think you're ahead, somewhere out of the blue, some witness makes an answer that knocks you back down. This was one of those days.

MacDonald had wept. The jury had wept. I felt like weeping, too, not from sympathy but frustration and pure anger. I was angry not at MacDonald but with the jury. I thought they were crying for him. Not until after the trial did I understand they were crying out of grief over the senselessness of Colette, Kimberly, and Kristen's deaths.

The next morning, I walked into the courtroom and saw the news crews that had been there for the entire trial, but today something different was happening. The case had taken on a national tone. The three television networks, CBS, ABC, and NBC, were there. I put my folders and papers on the prosecution table, turned, and quickly walked back upstairs.

Seeing no one in the hall, I ducked into the men's bathroom, locked the door, and threw up. I felt better. Later that morning at the break, one of the news reporters came up to me and marveled at how calm I was on such a day. I looked as though I could do this sort of thing with no sweat at all. I just looked at the man as if he was the dumbest person on earth.

There was never a chance that MacDonald would break on cross-examination. Our only objective was to put the crime scene and our evidence back in front of the jury and to do so without emotion. The previous day of direct examination had been an emotional roller coaster, and we did not want to play that game again.

Over and over, I asked MacDonald to assume certain facts about key points in evidence and then asked him if he had any explanation for that. I really didn't care what his answers were. I just wanted to remind the jury of the questions, which were the basis for the government's case.

For example, when I asked him why there was no Type B blood—his own—in the living room, his answer was that ice pick wounds, which he claimed he had, didn't bleed much. The problem with this answer appeared when I asked him to give me a time line, describing where he went in the apartment and when, after he woke up and found his family dead. He said it was about fifteen minutes before he went to the hall bathroom.

Now, a great deal of blood was found in that bathroom sink, and I asked him where that blood came from. His responded that he'd washed his hands because there was a lot of blood in the apartment that night. But the blood in the sink was Type B blood—his. So if the ice pick wounds did not bleed in the living room right after they were inflicted, how was it that they started bleeding some fifteen minutes after he woke up? How was it that Type B blood was found in the hall bathroom sink around the basin and just under the mirror? He had no satisfactory answer.

I asked MacDonald if he had any explanation for why blue-black cotton threads that matched his pajama top were found under Colette's body and under the headboard of their bed. He said no. What about the threads in Kristen's room? Any answer he gave would be pure conjecture, he said.

How did Type A blood (Colette's type) get on the bedsheet in the master bedroom and on the bottom of Colette's pajama bottoms, when she had no injuries to her legs? He couldn't answer, he said, because that would assume that the CID could properly type blood. And then I asked the question: but did your side object to any of the blood evidence coming before this jury? He had to answer . . . no.

Did he have any explanations for Type O (Kristen's type) on the floor in her bedroom? How about the fabric impressions on the bedroom sheet, which implied he'd carried Colette in the sheet from Kristen's bedroom back to the master bedroom? What about his footprint in Colette's Type A blood at the doorway to Kristen's room when there was no Type A blood on the floor *in* her room, only Type O? Is that when he stepped in his bare feet on the bedsheet before he carried Colette away and transferred the blood on the sheet to the floor? What about the smear of blood on the right cuff of his blue pajama top that even his own defense expert, John Thornton, said matched the blood found on the bedsheet? Did he do that, or did he have any explanation for how that blood got there? The answers to all these questions and more were no, no, no, he had no explanations.

The defense team believed at the end of the day that MacDonald had creamed us. Wade Smith told me to my face that he "was always pleased when a fellow member of the Bar does well." I later learned that, privately, he told his client that Blackburn "stoned you to death with popcorn."

But they would hear these questions and answers again in a few days, during the closing arguments. Then the popcorn would turn to hardballs.

Over the weekend, I was still concerned about the jury and the fact that they had cried during MacDonald's direct examination the previous Thursday. I was angry with the jury and wanted to tell them so. I called Ginny Carol, a reporter I knew at the local *News and Observer.* For about ten minutes I whined on the phone to her about the jury's tears and said that I intended to chastise them during closing arguments

Her reaction was swift. "Jim, if you do that, you will blow the whole case. That is about as stupid an idea as you've had this whole summer. Just forget about it, stick to your case, and give it your best shot. You've put on a strong case." I'm grateful she responded more as a friend than as a reporter.

That last weekend, I paced late at night in my backyard and tried to put everything in perspective. The trial had become more than just a case to me. I wanted to win, and I believed we had a chance to do so. Through the entire case we'd held our own. And we had done it with honor. But I knew that the greatest test had not yet come.

Closing arguments in criminal cases often draw people as though it's a special church service. At least in the South, it does. Jurors who dressed casually during the trial will show up in their dressiest new outfits. Men wear ties, and women wear jewelry and Sunday dresses.

Our jury consisted of seven men and five women. They had not been sequestered. No one was excused for any reason, and no one asked to have time off. No one was ever late, and there is no evidence any juror violated the oath of service in any way. They were the best jury I've ever watched at work.

On Monday evening, the night before the closing arguments began, I asked a clerk for the key to the courtroom across the hall from the one we were using. I went inside and locked the door. It was a twin of the other room, except it had no exhibits, no extra chairs, no hint of any drama. That night, I worked in there for about two hours. Alone, and for the only time, I practiced my closing remarks.

I don't think I was really alone. I sensed, as I reached the end, the spirit of three other people in that room—Colette, Kimberly, and Kristen. No one had yet really spoken for them, not even the government. We had shown the evidence that tied Jeffrey Mac-

Donald to their murders, but we had not yet captured what they lost, and what we lost by not knowing them. As if by magic, the words that I remember so well first came to me:

"If in the future, you should cry a tear, cry one for them.
If in the future, you should say a prayer, say one for them.
If in the future, you should light a candle, light one for them."

When I said those words in that empty courtroom that night, my voice broke. I knew then that I was ready.

That was a long time ago. Freddy and Mildred are dead. So is Jeffrey MacDonald's mother. Jeffrey MacDonald has grown twenty years older in prison. Witnesses, including Helena Stoeckley, have died. So, the question I ask myself now is, does anyone really care? That spring, one of his attorneys asked me, "Jim, isn't there some way Freddy and Jeff can make peace and bring this to an end, without there ever having to have a trial? After all, it's been almost ten years."

Did it make any difference whether the jury found MacDonald guilty? The answer is an overwhelming yes. That summer, justice was finally done in the Jeffrey MacDonald murder case.

I never met Colette, Kimberly, and Kristen. I never heard them speak. I only saw them in pictures in the scrapbooks that Freddy and Mildred showed me or in those awful pictures from the night of February 17, 1970. Yet I came to feel as if they were three of my closest friends.

I still know so much about them. I know their blood types as well as my own—better even than I know my own children's blood types. I have never forgotten the picture of the three caskets being carried into the chapel at Fort Bragg, with Jeffrey MacDonald walking in behind them, dressed in full uniform.

They were buried in Long Island, and a few years later, in the fall of 1974 when their bodies were exhumed to retrieve additional hair samples, the fact that Kimberly's and Kristen's graves had been reversed was discovered. Paul Stombaugh, the FBI agent

Left to right: Fellow prosecutor Brian Murtagh and I are surrounded by reporters after MacDonald verdict

who gathered the hair samples, identified Kimberly in part by noting which little girl's skull moved when he touched it. Only Kimberly's head would move in that way, because a club had found its mark years ago.

The most haunting picture of the entire trial is a black and white photograph of Kimberly that shows her whole face. She is lying undressed in the morgue. Despite the horror of her wound, you can still see how pretty she was, the long blonde hair, her gentle facial features. Death had come far too soon.

And little Kristen. The youngest one. Perhaps she died quickly. I hope so.

Twenty years have now passed since that summer. MacDonald is in federal prison and still maintains his innocence. He still attacks the government. The years have worn him and, late at night, he must wonder about the life he could have had and the medical work he could have performed. So much promise thrown away.

It's impossible to unring a bell, and I think that's why the girls were killed. I believe that MacDonald's motive for these terrible crimes was survival. The murders of the children, particularly Kristen, were committed to cover up the murder of his wife. Kimberly may have been struck at first accidentally, and she might have died from that wound alone, but the killer could not know that for certain. To make sure, her complete destruction was necessary.

One photograph shows an empty suitcase belonging to Jeffrey MacDonald, sitting on the floor near the foot of his bed. It is unlikely that the suitcase was there earlier in the evening, because it is between the wall and one side of the bed. Perhaps MacDonald intended at first to flee. Maybe he changed his mind and came up with the story of the hippie intruders. After all, the use of multiple weapons could suggest multiple attackers.

It is so much easier to blame someone else than to accept responsibility for oneself. No one could possibly think that a young, attractive doctor, a graduate of Princeton, who married his childhood sweetheart and was the father of two daughters, could ever take their lives.

I have lived with this case for so long that it has affected my very being. Yet, some things I still do not know. I don't know whether he finally killed Colette before stabbing Kristen. Only some bits of the latex gloves were found, what happened to the remnants? Why didn't he take the Valentine cards—the ones that said he was the "best daddy in the world"—with him when he left the apartment for good? He took the stereo, and he had a yard sale of some of his other belongings, making almost $3,500.

Where were the love letters he wrote to Colette? Why did we

only have ones from her to him and not the other way around? Didn't he write her any?

And why did he maintain that intruders came to his house to hurt him, because he wouldn't give drugs to people? If they were mad at him, why wasn't he killed but his family was? Why wasn't he hurt worse? Why was his family so destroyed? If the fight was in the living room, why was the evidence in the bedroom? Why did he lie so much about his injuries? And claim they were life threatening when they so clearly were not? His injuries required no stitches or bandages. He had only the collapsed lung on his right side, which was caused by an injury that the jury concluded he had inflicted himself.

Why didn't he let Kristen live? She was only two years old. Couldn't he have convinced her not to tell anyone? Had she even seen the murders? Maybe she didn't even know or wouldn't remember. Did he coldbloodedly decide she'd get in the way of a lifestyle he could now adopt as a single man?

Why did he tuck Kimberly and Kristen back in bed?

Was it worth it? Has MacDonald been happier since they died? Does he look forward to one day seeing them again? What will he say to them?

But really, what I want to know is why, why, why.

Flame-out

Why had Jeffrey MacDonald destroyed his family and himself, in a night so filled with arrogance, stupidity, selfishness, and brutality? That's the question that lingers after all these years. No one can answer it. I doubt they ever will.

The same question "Why" would be asked of me years later, when I destroyed my professional self just as surely as if I'd put a loaded gun to my head and fired. The destruction could not have been much worse.

After the MacDonald trial, I spent two additional years as a federal prosecutor, including one and a half years as the United States Attorney for North Carolina's Eastern District, which covers forty-four of the state's one hundred counties and reaches from Raleigh to North Carolina's coast.

After leaving the prosecutor's office, I specialized in criminal defense. I found that my winning streak in jury trials rapidly came to an end, or, as most defense attorneys will tell you, winning becomes a relative thing. Winning comes to mean probation rather than prison, conviction of a misdemeanor rather than a felony, getting life for your client rather than death. Rarely does winning become, Not Guilty. That is because most people who are charged with crimes are usually guilty of something, and the defense attorney's job is to make it as minor a something as possible.

In those years I developed an unnatural and unreasonable expectation of myself and what I could accomplish for my clients. I never wanted them to lose or be unhappy with the result of their case. Over time, I developed tremendous difficulty with telling some clients the bad news that they had no chance of winning a settlement or staying out of prison. I believed, sometimes unreasonably, that there was always hope.

I wanted to handle important matters, but importance, like beauty, is in the eye of the beholder. To every client, his or her case is the most important. There is no other. But to me, importance became something more. I was always trying to find the next MacDonald case and the publicity, complexity, and perhaps drama.

On January 13, 1993, I went to work at the law firm of Smith Helms Mulliss and Moore as I had for the past five and a half years. Smith Helms was a large firm in North Carolina with over 140 lawyers practicing in Charlotte, Greensboro, and Raleigh. It was managed by a policy committee of five attorneys from the various cities. I was one of the five.

That morning, I rode the elevator to the third floor, got off and turned left, walking back to my corner office. It was about 8:00 A.M. Within a few minutes, my telephone rang. I answered and heard the tense voice of a local bank employee who fired questions at me about a wire transfer of $50,000 from one of the firm's trust accounts to one of my clients in the northeast part of the state. I had authorized this transfer about six weeks before. She rapidly told me her superiors had questioned whether I had the authority to request the transfer, that it should not have been done, and that her job was in question. I told her everything was fine, that I would check into it and call her back immediately.

I sat back in my chair and tried to remain calm. Quickly, I dialed Steve Blackwell in Charlotte, the firm administrator, to find out what he knew. He refused to discuss my concern, telling me a lot of people were in his office, and that he'd get back to me. I didn't believe him.

Instinct told me to look out the window to the parking lot below. Quickly scanning the various cars that parked out front, I found it—a beige BMW convertible that belonged to one of the managing partners from Greensboro. That meant that Steve Earp was back in town and at our office.

Steve was a mild-mannered, sandy-haired environmental lawyer, who had developed a thriving practice over the last several years. He was considered to be one of the upcoming stars of the firm. But I had the uneasy feeling that Steve had not come so early to Raleigh to discuss environmental law. I believed he had come to see me.

Steve and Dick Ellis, another senior partner of the law firm and a former law school classmate of mine, called me into Dick's office. They slowly, painfully went over a number of irrefutable facts that included my setting up a case file for a matter that did not legally exist, my writing at least seventeen court orders of all kinds to resolve the alleged case, and then making a down payment to my clients of $50,000, which I'd wired to them almost two months ago on the Friday after Thanksgiving.

I remember sitting on the sofa in Dick's office. Dick was in the chair behind his desk, and Steve was off to the side. For as long as I could, I refuted their allegations. I tried to pretend everything I did was normal and proper. Finally, Dick looked squarely at me and said, "Jim, I just don't believe you. What I have read and what I have in my hands indicate to me that you have done wrong. Did you do these things?"

I sat quietly for a moment, looking at them. Finally I said, "Give me thirty seconds." I put my head down on my chest and closed my eyes. When I opened them, they were still there, still waiting for me to speak. This time I told them the truth. I had indeed done what they believed. I had wired money belonging to one client to another client. This is what I did.

I agreed to help a family I'd assisted several times before, this time in a land dispute with a neighbor. The case came to the firm in 1990. These clients lived in North Carolina, but they'd bought an empty lot at Lake Gaston in Virginia. The person who bought the lot next to them put up a boathouse and pier on land my clients thought belonged to them. Over a period of at least several months, I met with the family, spoke with them by telephone, and even visited their home in North Carolina twice. I visited the disputed vacation site in Virginia in July 1991. By fall 1991 I told them I'd filed a lawsuit.

For reasons that I wish I could explain, I never filed the complaint I prepared. After a period of time, with the complaint still not filed and the client demanding action, I went ahead and drafted orders as if the matter were a live case pending in a court of law. Over a good deal of time, I wrote seventeen court orders, forged various judges' signatures on them, and gave them to the family as if they were real.

They were seeking monetary damages, so I told the client that the Wake County Court had awarded them $250,000. But, of course, there was no such money, so I told them that the clerk of court had entered an order and someone took the money. Therefore a freeze had been placed on all bank accounts, I told them, and in a lawsuit at the appeals court—also fictitious, of course—they were again awarded $250,000.

Next I told my clients that the law firm had received the award, but the firm needed the money, and that's why they hadn't gotten it yet. Finally, after a great many telephone calls from them at my office and even at home, demanding the money they believed had been awarded them, I decided to send them $50,000 as a down payment. On the day after Thanksgiving, last year, I'd had lunch with my father, Glenn, and my older brother, Glenn, Jr. I told them I had to leave before 2:00 P.M. to wire some money to a client. I drove to the office, asked a partner if I had the authority to wire money from the firm's Raleigh trust account, and then I called the bank and did so. That was the transfer that blew the case up in my face.

I think back to that time now and wish that I could change everything. I wish that I had walked into Dick's office long before and told him the truth. I wish I'd told the truth earlier that very day. But I didn't. I believed that my survival as an attorney was at stake, and therefore I acted wrongly and kept quiet. My survival as a person required something very different, however, and that became even more important than saving my career as a lawyer.

What a day. We'd been friends and now our conversation was strained. Before Dick could tell me to leave the firm, I told him I knew what needed to be done, that he didn't have to ask me. The conversation wound down. Steve suggested he and I go for a walk downtown.

Outside I said, "I can't believe all this is happening to me, Steve, I just can't. Do you think I should resign from the law firm?"

"Yes, Jim, I do. The whole thing is amazing to me, but I don't think you have much choice."

"I understand. Do you mind walking downtown?"

"No, I think that a good walk would help us both. I just wanted you to get out of the building at this point."

We walked across the capitol grounds, silent statues surrounding us, the grass still green even in winter. Just the two of us, in business suits with no overcoats, on a walk in the middle of a sunny afternoon in January. Nothing looked abnormal.

Soon we neared the offices of the North Carolina State Bar, where we spotted Bob Wicker, a tall dark-haired man with whom I'd also been in law school. A law partner of ours in Greensboro, he was just beginning a year's term as the president of the state bar.

"Hey, Jim, I thought I might run into you, but I was hoping I wouldn't."

"I know, Bob, I know. I want you to know how sorry I am about all of this."

"I know you are. I want you to know that I still consider you my friend."

"Thanks. Steve and I are going for a walk and talking things over. I'll see you soon."

We walked a little further. Around the corner, I spotted former U.S. Senator Robert Morgan walking toward us. Senator Morgan had been my longtime mentor as a lawyer. He'd given me my first job as a lawyer, right out of law school.

"Damn it, Steve, there's Senator Morgan. Let's go the other way. I don't think I can deal with this just now."

"Sure, Jim, you lead the way."

I wish we could have kept on walking and never gone back. But as the hour grew late, we found ourselves back in the parking lot outside our office. The Raleigh office of Smith Helms Mulliss and Moore was a beautiful and stately three-story brick building that took up almost an entire lot. For me it had represented my professional work, where I spent a lot of my time, and where a lot of my friends were. I had been at home there.

But now, I did not want to go back inside. No one had to tell me. I knew. My time at the firm was over.

In looking back on that day, I understand now how life should be lived. Life needs to be lived fully and with friends. Living a good life means taking care of each other, being gracious to those in distress, compassionate, just and fair. Life is for holding hands and loving each other. Because in a moment, all that makes us content can dissipate and life will never be the same. The greatest sadness would be if we missed our chance to appreciate what we had while we had it.

What's the Worst You've Done?

I left Smith Helms that afternoon and headed home. I could not put off telling my family what had happened to me . . . and now to them. On my way home, driving through Raleigh's neighborhoods, I called my friend Wade Smith, whom I'd gotten to know well when he assisted in the defense of Jeffrey MacDonald in 1979.

Wade, older than I am, had been an all-conference football player at the University of North Carolina under the legendary coach, Jim Tatum. He'd been a Morehead scholar while he was there, a great academic honor, and was a co-founder of his well-established law firm many years ago. Wade was a big fellow, barrel-chested, with thinning gray hair. He exuded a warm embrace of the human spirit, which reached all those he met. Wade had been my friend for many years, and I wanted to talk to him.

The phone rang, and his secretary answered. "Jan, this is Jim. Is Wade there? I need to speak to him immediately."

Wade came on the line. "Hello, JB, what's up?"

"Wade, I'm in trouble. I have done some bad things. I've left the firm."

"When?"

"Just now. I'm on the way home to tell Marsha."

"Jim, have you done anything criminal?"

Left to right: Wade Smith and me, several years ago. We argued opposite sides of many well-publicized cases over the years. How ironic that my best opponent became one of my best defenders.

"No, I don't think so, but I have done a number of stupid things involving some cases and clients."

"Are you getting ready to run off with a blonde?"

I started to laugh. "No, Wade, I'm not doing that."

"Good. Anything else we can handle."

"Wade, I need to talk to you right away. Can you meet me?"

"Yes, I can leave the office now and meet you in thirty min-utes."

We met at a local restaurant in a small shopping center about two miles from my house. It was about 4 P.M., and I got there first.

Wade soon arrived, wearing a dark blue suit, an overcoat, and hat, and carrying a well-worn briefcase. When he saw me, he walked up and gave me a big bear hug and motioned me to one of the back booths.

The waitress came over and Wade told her, "Two coffees and a lot of patience. We're going to be here awhile."

He got out his legal pad and pen, looked at me, and said, "Jim, tell me the worst thing you have done that you can think of."

"I sent money from one of the firm's trust accounts to a client of mine. It wasn't their money."

"Whose money was it?"

"It belonged to another client of mine. He had $57,000 in one of our trust accounts."

"Does this other person know about this?"

"No, he doesn't. But I'm going to tell him, and I want to do that before the firm does."

"Okay, Jim, what else?"

"Well, there's another client. Just before Christmas, he needed some money, and I sent him $6,000 from that same trust account. I left $1,000 in there. It's still there."

"Okay, that's $56,000. What else?"

"There was this case, or sort of this case. It was one that I had never filed. I don't really know why I didn't, but I didn't. I let the clients think it had been filed and that, after a long period of time, they won the case. Of course, they wanted their money. That's where the $50,000 comes in. That was part of their 'recovery'.

"I wrote a bunch of orders, I don't know how many and don't even remember what they all said. But the upshot was that after a fictitious protracted legal battle, they had been successful."

"Who signed these orders, Jim? Did you?"

"Yeah, I signed them. Wrote them too. They weren't too good.

I signed different judge's names to them. I didn't try to disguise my handwriting or anything. I just signed the name of whomever came to mind when I was writing them."

"Okay, what else?"

"Wade, there's more that I need to tell you, but that is all I am up to today. I'll tell you more later."

"Okay, Jim, I think I understand. I want you to know that we're going to work this out, this is not the end for you. You have a whole life ahead of you. I'm going to help you, and I want you to know that you will never owe me one dime. I want no fee."

I just looked back at him in relief. "Wade, that's wonderful. Of course, you know I have no money anyway."

He laughed but quickly turned serious. "Jim, the first thing we need to do is get you examined by a doctor, a psychiatrist. I know the best one in the world. We need to see if she can see you this week, tomorrow if possible."

"You really think I need that? I've never been to one of those doctors before in my life. Are you sure?"

"I'm positive. Look, we need to see if there's something wrong with you that might explain your recent behavior. I've known you too long, Jim, to think that you'd do these things without some explanation. These actions are bizarre, they're out of character for you.

"The truth is that you may not be well. I don't know. But I do know that the first thing we need to do is take care of you and your health. That is the most important thing. The rest of this stuff can wait. You're no good to anybody if you're not in good health."

"Wade, I'm not sure about going to a psychiatrist. I don't really want to do that."

"Jim, I feel strongly that you need to see one. Dr. Jean Spaulding can help you if anyone can. You'll be able to talk to her in complete confidence. I have no doubt that you need to do that."

"Who's Jean Spaulding?"

"Just the best doctor I know. The first thing I'm going to do when I get back to the office is call her and see about getting you an appointment tomorrow or the next day."

"Okay, Wade, if that's what you think I should do, I'll do it. What do I do now, tomorrow, next week? I don't have a job any more, or at least not for a few days."

"I think you need to take some time off. You have been at this for a long time. You need to get away by yourself. Go hiking. Try to walk part of the Appalachian Trail. Ride your bike across part of the country and keep a journal of everything that happens to you. Jim, what I'm saying is that you need to rest and let us figure out what has gone wrong. Then we can fix it. But Jim, something has gone wrong."

"Do you think I can work this out? You think I can survive this? I have pretty much screwed things up."

"Your career has gone a little off track. But you can come back. You can be okay again. You're strong. And you are a good person."

"Thanks, Wade. I guess I need to go home and talk to Marsha. She needs to know. I really do not want to do this."

"Do you want me to go with you?"

"No, I should do this myself. I can do it. I'll be okay."

I watched Wade walk to his car, putting on his hat as he did so. I took a deep breath, opened the restaurant door, and walked into the cooling air for the short ride home.

Wade was already in an active legal defense mode. He had no idea why I had done the things I'd told him, and I don't believe he knew whether Dr. Jean Spaulding could help me. Whenever he had a client who had done something terribly wrong, his immediate response was to seek psychiatric assistance. He did this to discover a medical explanation for the wrongdoing, if possible, in case he could build a medical defense of the conduct that might prove helpful in subsequent legal proceedings. He needed evidence in my case, and Dr. Spaulding was the first stop along the way.

Opening the door to my house, I saw Marsha and our two

One year before flame-out. My loyal family, *left to right:* Jeff, Stacy, and Marsha

children, Jeff and Stacy, in the kitchen. Jeff was a high school senior and Stacy was in the eighth grade. They had just gotten home from school and were preparing an afternoon snack.

One look at me and they all knew something was wrong. "Marsha, we need to talk. Let's go for a walk."

She quickly put on her coat and we went outside. As we walked up the sidewalk on a major street not far from our home, I began, in halting words, to tell her what had happened to me that day.

"Marsha, there's no easy way to tell you this, but I am going to have to leave the law firm."

She was incredulous. "Why? What on earth for?"

"Well, I've done some stupid things. I transferred a lot of money from one of the firm's trust accounts to some clients. About $50,000."

"You did what? To those people who call here all the time? Why? Have you lost your mind?"

"Well, they thought they were entitled to it, so I sent it to them."

"What does the firm think about that?"

"They're not happy about it."

"Can any of this be fixed? Is it for sure that you're going to have to leave the firm?"

"No, I don't think it can be fixed. Yes, I think it's definite I have to leave. In fact, everyone is probably being told about it right now."

We walked in silence for a time. I was still dressed in a dark pin-striped suit and black wingtip shoes. People driving by seemed to be looking at us strangely. I'm sure I did not look like I was out for a casual walk.

Finally, Marsha looked at me and asked me, "What do you want me to do?"

I was not sure I knew what she meant.

"I mean, what do you want the children and me to do?" she said. "Do you want us to stay around or go and leave you alone or what?"

"Marsha, I know this is not what you signed on for, so I would understand if you wanted to leave. But I would like for you to stay."

"Okay, then I'll stay. You know, they said for better or for worse. We've had better, now I guess it's time for worse."

We held hands and slowly made our way back home. Because Jeff was still in exams, we agreed not to say anything to him and Stacy until the end of the week.

The next afternoon, I met with my FBI agent friend and told him what had happened to his money. I assured him his money was now safe because the firm had immediately replaced it. He was understanding and said he wished I'd told him earlier so that he could have helped me in some way. He told me he was thankful I'd spoken to him when I did.

That evening, I told Jeff and Stacy about what had happened and that I would be leaving the firm. I remember sitting in a chair in our upstairs bedroom talking to Stacy. She was very calm and understanding, but tears began to slide down her face.

Meeting Doctor Spaulding

The next day, I met Dr. Jean Spaulding for my first appointment. Her office was in Durham, about twenty miles from Raleigh. I walked up to her Dutch Colonial office, which resembled a typical neighborhood home, complete with front yard and brick sidewalk.

I really did not want to see a psychiatrist. My original appointment was for the day before, but I'd canceled. On Friday, the law firm asked if I wanted someone to go over there with me. They had someone follow me to make sure I went.

If they had not done that, I would never have made it to Dr. Spaulding's office. I did not want to open up to anyone, much less a total stranger. I didn't think anything was wrong with me mentally that required a psychiatrist. I was doing this because my good friend Wade had almost required me to go. Unemployed as an attorney and facing God knows what, I was not in a strong position, so I did as I was told. Later I would learn that over the preceding three to four years, Wade Smith had frequently expressed to Dr. Spaulding his concern about "my good friend Jim" and his repeated desire that I receive some therapy.

Jean Spaulding is a strikingly attractive African-American woman, well dressed and well mannered, with a compassionate manner. We talked for about an hour. I sat in a low chair facing her blonde wood desk, behind which she sat taking notes as we

Dr. Jean Spaulding, my psychiatrist, saved my life

talked. The room was quiet, the mood confidential. Glass panels that made up two of the walls were well draped, and the carpet was a calming mauve.

"What can I do for you?"

"I've had a bad day."

"That's what Wade told me."

"What do you want to know?"

"We've got forty-five minutes. Why don't you just start at the beginning. Tell me everything. Don't leave anything out."

I found it difficult to open up. I was not used to telling anyone my problems or admitting that I had done anything wrong. I had spent my professional life trying to solve other people's problems and often listening to them tell me what they had done wrong.

I told Dr. Spaulding what had taken place over the last several days at the law firm, and my actions that had led up to this week. She didn't ask many questions that day, but mainly listened, nodding earnestly and taking notes. Her voice was smooth and radiated understanding. She seemed sympathetic.

The conversation began this way, " Jim, when did you leave the firm?"

"About three hours ago."

"Why are you not working there any more?"

"You really want to know?"

She smiled again, "I really want to know."

"Well, I've done some really stupid things, I mean really dumb. A few weeks ago, I transferred $50,000 to some clients out of our firm's trust account. It wasn't their money. It belonged to someone else I knew, who was also a client of mine. You're not supposed to do that. I know that. I've always known that. But I did it."

"Why did you do it?"

"They wanted it. They thought they were entitled to money. They got that notion from me. You see, they have a lot on Lake Gaston in Virginia. The person who bought the lot next to theirs put a boathouse and pier on a location that my clients thought belonged to them. They wanted it removed.

"My clients live in North Carolina, and I had helped both of them and their two children in other legal matters over the years, so they called me. It should have taken very little time and very little effort, or I should not have taken the case at all."

"Why did you take the case then?"

"I don't know. I just couldn't tell them no. I'd known them for a long time. I helped the wife when she had, uh, something at the Department of Motor Vehicles. I met the son because he had a ticket. I did a ticket for the daughter and a ticket for the father. They were in a swim club and got behind on the dues, so I paid $1,500 of my personal money to catch them up on their dues. I even made a talk, in about 1985, for the daughter about MacDonald.

"This case started in spring 1990. Nothing happened for over a year. Finally in July 1991, I met them at Lake Gaston and promised to help them. That fall, I let them think I'd filed a lawsuit for them. I hadn't, though I had prepared one to file. I don't know why I never filed it. That would have been too easy, I suppose.

"Anyway, they of course wanted to know what was happening and nothing had. But I told them it had, and it went on and on from there."

I told her of writing the phony orders, though I was quick to tell her that none of them were ever filed in any court. Somehow I thought that fact might save me.

"Tell me about these orders you said you wrote. How did you get them signed?"

"I signed them for the judges."

"You signed judges' names?"

"Yes, I did."

"How did you decide which judges to use?"

"I don't know. I really don't. I knew a lot of judges and just used whatever name came to mind. I tried to be consistent, but that's about it. I knew all the North Carolina judges, most of them have been friends of mine."

I told her that my client got so angry he wanted to go out and shoot the neighbor. To prevent this, I'd told my client that the neighbor had fired a shot toward my clients' property, and I had the bullet to prove it.

"Actually I showed him an old bullet that I had in my desk that I'd gotten from an FBI agent. I thought that was the best of all the tales and I told many tales."

Dr. Spaulding looked up at me sharply and wrote furiously on her pad. She told me later that my calm demeanor when making this comment about telling tales indicated that I did not yet comprehend the depth of my psychological problems.

I finished the story. "I told my clients that the guy had been prosecuted but there would be no sentence in that case. Eventually, I gave the clients an order that said they were entitled to $250,000."

"Two hundred fifty thousand dollars? Do you know whose name you used to sign that order?"

"I don't know."

"How were these people going to get this amount of money?"

"All of it, I don't know, but I did get them some of it. When I couldn't hold them off any longer, I wired them $50,000 from the firm's trust account as a partial settlement in the case. They were driving me crazy about it; the husband was calling me every day, two or three times a day. I had to call him every night. Always about the money and always about the fact that the boathouse and pier hadn't been removed. He was obsessed about that and I guess I got obsessed with his obsession. I would tick off three or four different things I was working on for him simultaneously in every single phone call.

"He'd constantly respond, 'That will be good.' I'd get off the phone and feel pretty good for a second, and then I'd have to call him back. I called him at his motel room so often I knew his number by heart. They even got upset and called me on Sundays at home when they saw the person who had built the boathouse and pier had cut the grass."

"They got upset about that? Why?"

"I suppose because it showed evidence of ownership and trespassing on my clients' property. Probably all it did was cut down on the presence of snakes. You see, my clients' property was vacant. Tall grass and an undisturbed lot would be a haven for snakes."

"Where does the $50,000 come in?"

"That was their first down payment."

"And that money came from the firm's trust account?"

"That's right."

"Why did you send that to them if you knew that was wrong?"

"That's a good question. I didn't think about it being right or wrong. That never entered my mind at all. I knew that I needed to send them some money, and that I could send this money. It was that simple. They were entitled to it, and there it was. I wired it. Of course, they weren't really entitled to the money, but at that time I thought they were. I had been doing this so long and having so many conversations with them that it became real to me. When I spoke to them, we would even talk strategy. It was like flicking a light switch on and off."

"How did you feel after you wired the money?"

"I felt great, a sense of relief. The rest of the day was okay. It was a lot better than two days before when one of the clients called me at home and was extremely ugly to me, cursing a lot. He yelled at me throughout the entire conversation. I was an hour or so late calling him that day and that upset him. After I wired the money, I actually felt I'd done the firm a favor because I was protecting it. Sending those clients $50,000 was much better than the clients taking legal action against the firm."

"Who has the money now?"

"The clients do, I suppose. Then there's a second thing I should tell you about."

"What's that?"

"I had another client, a similar sort of thing only I didn't sign any orders for him. He thought he was owed some money also. I sent him about $6,000 right before Christmas. He owed some money he had borrowed, about $2,000. His wife had been sick, and he needed money for Christmas. The man he owed was hot on him for it. I made sure he had some. I think it was three days before Christmas. Talked to him on the phone and he was real happy. Said I had taken a real load off him. I'd already given him money about a year ago. Said he was grateful and would never forget me. I suppose he won't."

"Where did this $6,000 come from?"

"It was part of $57,000 that I knew was in the firm's trust account. I left $1,000 alone."

"You wired $56,000 of the $57,000 in the trust account, and you didn't think it would be noticed?"

"I wasn't really thinking about it being noticed. That wasn't first on my mind."

"What was?"

"Getting those people to stop calling me . . . just for a day."

At this point, Dr. Spaulding looked down at her desk, and I looked at my watch. It was 3:30 P.M., half of my time was gone. I was more relaxed than when I first got there. Then she got personal.

"Jim, I need to ask you whether there's any history of drug abuse in your life?"

"What are you asking?"

"Have you ever used cocaine, or are you now using any form of cocaine?"

"No, that's easy to answer. The answer to both questions is no."

"No cocaine?"

"No cocaine."

"You don't mind being tested for that?"

"No, I don't mind, whenever you want."

The personal questions about my background continued for the remainder of my session. I thought I did rather well. Only years later did I learn that Jean Spaulding thought my behavior that day was hardly appropriate for my circumstances; that is, I smiled too much as I talked, and I didn't appear to understand the seriousness of my situation. I didn't comprehend the fact that my professional career was going up in flames. Instead of showing anxiety, I'd smiled and spoken quite matter-of-factly about irrational reasons for actions that were really crimes.

In truth, I was in denial. This was not the first time, nor would it be the last, that I wore the mask of comedy rather than tragedy. It was simply the way I knew to cope . . . to survive. I'd never bared my soul to anyone, and all my defenses were up that day. For a long time in my sessions with Jean Spaulding, I resisted surrendering my thoughts and feelings. To do so would indicate weakness, I feared, and I was obsessed with not being perceived that way. That was more important to me than finding out the truth about what caused my conduct. It was also the greatest impediment to my getting well.

I alternated between states of devastation and denial. I still thought of myself as an attorney, just one without a current job. Like being on a raft on a swirling river, I just wanted to stay afloat. I knew it would be a long time coming before the water flowed calmly again.

I didn't totally trust Jean Spaulding or anyone else at that time. I always kept information and thoughts in reserve. I felt that if anyone knew the whole me, then that person would deem me completely unworthy. So keeping part of me locked inside was essential to being liked and well regarded, even by my own doctor.

My father was a Baptist minister and had spent a lifetime dealing with families in times of extreme emotion. He had performed countless weddings of happiness and also countless funerals with great sadness. Somehow, he had learned the traits of calmness and decency in such times, and he had passed on at least the semblance of those traits to me. Outwardly at least, I was calm and in control.

Inwardly was another matter. Dr. Spaulding sensed that what she saw on the surface was not my true self. Through her professional experience, she knew that it was difficult to take a fall as steep as mine without my possibily taking action to stop my pain. She was concerned about keeping me alive long enough to find out what was wrong. She asked me if I had any suicidal thoughts.

"Yeah, I've thought about it," I answered, "but I don't know how I'd do it. We don't have any guns at home, and I'm afraid of knives. I don't like heights. I have considered walking into traffic, but, with my luck, I would only be hurt and not killed. I'd wind up a vegetable and be totally humiliated. So, I don't know."

What she said next brought me up short. "You need to know, Jim, that if you should do something to yourself, there's a good chance that one of your children will likely do the same thing when they reach your age. It's not certain, but the odds go way up. You should think about that."

I stared at her, stunned.

Dr. Spaulding ordered drug screening and psychological tests for me and gave me a small number of Prozac pills. She would not prescribe too many at once for fear I'd take them all at once. She had Marsha scour our house to eliminate any items I could use to take my life.

I was confused. I knew that I had done wrong, but I didn't know why. The sessions with Dr. Spaulding made me feel better. I didn't know going to a psychiatrist could be a pleasant experience. I found that talking to someone about my life and problems, assured of the doctor-patient confidentiality, was helpful. I found at the end of each session that I felt relaxed and more in control of my life as I drove back home.

Show Me the Money

On Wednesday of the following week, I called Dick Ellis at the firm. He had scheduled a late afternoon meeting with some clients of mine to discuss the future handling of their son's case, which involved a first- degree murder charge. It was readily apparent from a reading of the billing and accounts receivable sheets that the money they paid had not been credited to their account.

"Jim, do you know where that money is? Did you work those hours or put the money in your pocket?"

I took a deep breath. "Dick, lets talk somewhere in person, this afternoon if we can."

"I can meet now for a few minutes. Where do you want to meet?"

"I don't know. How about the parking lot across the street from the 42nd Street Oyster Bar? That's just a couple of blocks from your office."

"Okay. I'll see you there in twenty minutes."

It was a very cold, windy day. The parking lot was empty except for my car as I waited for Dick to appear. Shortly he drove up, put on a brown trench overcoat, and, with his yellow pad in hand, got out of his car.

"Dick, let's talk for a few minutes without anyone taking notes."

He hesitated. "Jim, you know I'm going to have to do that shortly."

"I understand that, but let me at least get started first."

He put away the pad.

"I guess you want to know if I took any money?"

"Yes, Jim, I do."

"You know, it's funny, in a way. Here I am, a criminal defense lawyer, getting ready to talk to someone about doing something wrong, and although I've met with Wade Smith, I haven't talked to him about the specifics yet."

"Jim, I've wondered about that. Don't start talking to me if you feel like you need to go over this with Wade first."

I thought for a long moment. Finally, I looked at Dick and said "No, I'll talk to you. The answer is yes, with some clients, over a period of time, I did take some money. I also paid a lot of money out to other clients, money they thought they deserved."

"Do you remember which clients you took money from?"

"Probably. I'd have to think about it for awhile, but I'll meet with you, say, tomorrow morning and tell you as specifically as I can."

"Would you do that? If you will, that's great. But if not, I would rather continue talking now."

"No, I'll meet you tomorrow for breakfast."

And our meeting was over. I'd talked with a man I'd gone to law school with, someone who had trusted me completely in the affairs of the law firm, and I'd told him about stealing money—violations of criminal law—and asked questions about the district attorney and the state bar. I had admitted, even more so than the previous week, wrongdoings that were rapidly changing my life.

It didn't make much difference to me that day whether the money had gone to me for selfish reasons or through me to others for some misguided purpose. Taking money is wrong. I'd done it, and people were going to find out about it. I had signed judges' names to fictitious orders, and some people already knew about that. I had not told the truth to various clients, and they either now knew that or soon would.

For some reason, I kept on going. I had no plan, except now I'd tell the truth. I tried not to stop and think about the consequences of what I was now doing or saying. I just kept to the plan: tell the truth.

I met again with the firm's lawyers and told them in detail as much as I could remember about everything that I had done. I had not only wired money to two separate clients, totaling $56,000, I had caused an additional $22,000 plus to be sent to the United States government to assist another client who owed money. Finally, I told them, as they surely now knew, that I had deposited fees from clients into my personal checking account, and subsequently I wrote large numbers of checks from that account to other clients as well.

A Major Depression

Initially, I didn't believe in psychiatry. I didn't believe in medication for depression or, for that matter, in depression itself. I thought of depression as an excuse people used for either wrongdoing or the inability to function well in society. I thought people who were depressed were weak. I thought that if you just pulled yourself up by your bootstraps and got on with it, you would be all right.

The first week after I met Jean Spaulding, Wade started hinting gently that he thought I should check myself into a hospital that had a psychiatric wing. I immediately rejected his suggestion. Surely that was not necessary. I thought psychiatric hospitalization was an extreme action reserved only for those people who were truly sick. I was not convinced that I was.

Jean now expressed some reservations about my immediate future. "Jim, I am concerned, and I have discussed this with Wade, about your ability to handle the publicity that is likely to come from your actions. You are a well-known attorney. You prosecuted the MacDonald case, and everybody in this part of the country knows about that. So what has happened to you is likely to be in the paper."

"Jean, what are you saying to me?"

"We need to think this through very carefully, but we may want to consider placing you in a hospital very soon."

"A hospital? Why?"

"We want you to be safe and very private if this information should come out. We want to protect you. At the same time, while you are there, we can have you thoroughly examined from head to toe. Perhaps we could find some reasons why all of this has occurred."

"Wade's mentioned the hospital idea to me, but I told him it wasn't necessary, that he was out of his mind. I can't conceive of myself being in a hospital. What kind of hospital?"

"Well, one that has a psychiatric wing. That's where you need to be. Nearby so I can get to you at any time. It needs to be away from Raleigh, perhaps here in Durham. You don't need any extra publicity, and you need to be kept as quiet as possible."

On Friday afternoon, I found myself in Rick Gammon's office, another well-known attorney in Raleigh. Rick was a young, well-built man with short brown curly hair. He had once been a Raleigh police officer before going to law school. Like Wade, I trusted him completely. We had practiced law together for several years in the early 1980s, and we had remained close friends ever since. Last week, I'd reached out to him soon after talking to Wade that first afternoon, and he'd taken me for a ride.

As we'd driven around Raleigh, I told him that I had to leave the law firm because of what I'd done. I'd suggested, half jokingly, that perhaps we should just bolt and go to the beach that very minute.

There was no hesitation in Rick's voice. "Listen, man, if that's what you want, I'll call the office, clear my calendar, and we can go right now."

But we didn't go, and this afternoon, days later, I was nearing the bottom of my life, or so I thought. I found that telling the truth about wrongdoing is very difficult the first time. And I did not tell it all at once. It was gradual. I'm not sure I could have done it any other way. I was not positive I could admit to myself all that I had done, so it was very hard for me to tell other people. But they gave me the time I needed.

As Rick and I talked in his private law office high atop one of Raleigh's tallest buildings, I again felt concerned about other people finding out what I had done. The state bar was on the verge of filing a complaint against me in superior court and obtaining a restraining order, which would prevent me from handling any client funds. The practical effect of these actions is that they'd keep me from practicing law. I was not as concerned about the practice of law as I was about the filing of a lawsuit, which would soon become public.

"Jim, you can't prevent this," Rick warned me. "I think the bar is determined to move ahead. They do it every time a trust account is involved. They have no choice, in their minds."

"But they know I'm not practicing law now, and they know where I am. If they do this, the whole world is going to find out."

"Jim, you cannot protect yourself or your family from the hurt that is getting ready to come."

"Yes, I can."

"How?"

"I can take a pass, that's how. That way, I'm still a lawyer, and they can just print that I'm dead. There won't be so much interest in the other stuff."

"You're not thinking straight, Jim. We have been through too much together for you to do something like that. You can survive this. We just have to find out how."

"I don't know, Rick. This is pretty bad. I think I'll go home."

"Look, Jim, I don't want to get a phone call in the middle of the night telling me I no longer have a friend. I don't want that."

"I understand. Thanks."

Not until years later did I learn that for several days and nights, Rick had me tailed to make sure I didn't go off in the woods somewhere and try to end my life.

That night Marsha and I were standing in the kitchen, and I told her about the suggestion that I enter a hospital very soon. She agreed completely. I was stunned. I didn't know anyone who was close to me who thought I was okay. Everyone thought I was ill. I knew I had done wrong, but I was still not convinced that anything was mentally wrong with me.

"What does your father think?" I asked her.

"There's no doubt in his mind. He thinks you are very sick and need treatment."

When I learned that Marsha agreed with Wade and Jean that I needed hospitalization, I knew that I had to surrender to this idea and go. I'm glad I did. Later I learned that they were prepared to have me sent there, without my agreement, if that was necessary. I'm glad I'd spared them that.

Unconditional love is the best and perhaps the rarest gift in the world. Nothing else comes close. I was lucky enough during those days to have Marsha and my children, who never wavered, and two friends for lawyers, Wade and Rick, who were frantically trying to help me without asking anything in return. I was lucky, too, to find Jean Spaulding, who quickly became my good friend as well as my doctor. They were a small band but a fiercely protective one.

Within twenty-four hours, everyone agreed that I should voluntarily commit myself to Duke University Medical Center's psychiatric wing. On Saturday afternoon, after a morning meeting with Jean Spaulding and a long walk with Marsha, I met with Wade and Rick at Wade's law office.

As we prepared for the week ahead, Wade closed the meeting by recounting the story in the movie *Arthur*. "You remember the scene after Arthur's prospective father-in-law kicks the hell out of him, Arthur stands at the front of the church and addresses all the guests?"

Wade stood up, pulled his tie to one side, mussed up his hair, and mimicked Arthur's words. "I want you to know, ladies and gentlemen, I'm not going to be seeing you for awhile. I'm going to the hospital, and when I get out, I'm going to be rather poor, so we won't be going to the same places. So I want to take this opportunity to tell you good-bye."

Rick and I looked at him in amazement and burst out laughing. "You think I should make that speech, right?"

"Well, Jim, it's something we might want to consider. It might get some laughs."

"I have no doubt."

I was the first to leave. As I did I said, "Listen, guys, there's one thing I want. When I walk out of this room, I don't want the two of you to look at each other and start laughing and saying things like 'can you believe this.' Please don't do that."

"Jim, this is a serious moment. A sad moment. We wouldn't think of doing that. We are putting everything we have into this for you, and we are just as serious about this as we can be."

"Wade, you forget who you're talking to. I've been in this situation too many times myself. Trust me, I know how it is."

"Jim, believe me, we're not laughing, not for a minute."

"Okay. I'll see the two of you sometime. I guess it's off to Duke on Monday."

I walked out the door and went home for the weekend.

Locked in a Psychiatric Ward

The decision to go to a psychiatric hospital is not an easy one. To admit that you need help in dealing with your problems—indeed in staying alive—is overwhelming. At least it was for me. By the weekend before I went to Duke, however, I was ready to go. In going, I agreed to surrender all control of movement, treatment, and medication. In going, I acknowledged that quite frankly I needed help; I could no longer cope safely on my own.

I did not know how long I would stay. Dr. Jean Spaulding had talked in terms of weeks, but hospital insurance cut that down to one. I didn't know whether Dr. Spaulding would allow me to return home when I was released, or if she'd want me to stay in Durham in case I needed to see her immediately. This was, in fact, a question in play until the very end.

When I went into the hospital, no one except for family and close friends knew I was going or that anything was all that wrong with me. I did not know what the public would know when I was released, but I knew that my fifteen minutes of fame from the MacDonald case had now been extended.

Helplessness is one feeling that comes to mind when I recall my hospitalization. Overwhelming sadness is another. The need for safety was paramount, however, and I have no doubt today that my hospital stay played a major role in keeping me alive. I could not harm myself, and the locked hospital doors kept the world outside and away.

Marsha agreed, though she was quite frightened, that hospitalization was essential. Everyone knew, and had accepted the inevitable except, that is, me. Marsha and I talked with Dr. Spaulding. She told us that my depression, the allegations that would appear in the press, as well as the mounting pressures of the entire situation made it imperative that I be hospitalized for my own safety.

We understood what had to be done. Marsha wept openly while I struggled to keep my tears from spilling over. Only after Marsha stepped outside to wait in the waiting room could I put my head in my hands and cry. I remember speaking to Jean in a hushed voice about how my life—all the work, all the hours of study, the legal arguments, innumerable legal briefs, all my political aspirations—had been reduced to this one moment of despair. I felt I could not go on.

I entered Duke University Medical Center, which is a teaching hospital. At any time a number of medical students might march into your room with a doctor and ask questions. I had just made up my bed and was lying on it, looking at the ceiling, when my first group appeared.

They interviewed me: How was I doing? Why was I there? What had I done? What medication was I on? Did I want to talk to anyone? For a short while, I was polite and tried to answer all their questions. Then I rebelled and shut down. I stayed on my bed and closed my eyes. I refused to meet any other patients. I did not want a walking tour of the place. I would not talk with the doctors. I wanted to be left alone. Finally, I was.

Lights-out happened at about ten o'clock every night. My solid wood door was pushed shut, but someone opened it every fifteen minutes and looked inside to make sure I was sleeping in my bed. Early every morning, a very pleasant nurse came in to check my pulse, temperature, and blood pressure. She'd tell me to have a blessed day and leave without another word.

That first morning, I walked slowly, very slowly, out my door and up the hall. Breakfast had been announced and I was hungry. I got the tray with my name on it and walked to a table to join several others who were sitting there in their bathrobes, some with blank stares that were now directed squarely at me.

I was nervous. This was the day after the state bar filed its complaint, and I assumed the Raleigh paper would publish a story about me. I wanted to read it and see how bad it was, even though I knew it would make me feel worse. It would also make everything more real to me, however. Now, the world would know part of what I had done.

After breakfast, I walked to the main station and asked one of the nurses how I could get a newspaper.

"Let's see, you're Mr. Blackburn, aren't you. Hmmm . . . that's what I was afraid of. Someone's going to have to go with you to get a paper. We can't let you go by yourself."

"Why's that?"

"We rate every person who comes in here on a scale from one to five. One means you can't ever go anywhere, and five means you can leave on your own with no supervision."

"What am I?"

"You are a three. That means you cannot leave this ward without someone with you at all times. They don't want you outside this ward by yourself."

"I see."

"I tell you what. A group of smokers are going out in about half an hour, and they'll be supervised. You can go with them. We'll let you know when it's time."

"Okay, thanks." I walked back to my room dejectedly and lay back down on my bed. The day before, I had learned that all personal items, such as razors and belts, had to be locked up. I had to have permission to get them back, and then I could use them only for a short time. Now, I realized that even my freedom to go get a newspaper was restricted. My world, like that of all the others here, was reduced to a few rooms and short halls.

When I was called to go outside, I scrambled out of my room and joined three or four others who were going out to smoke. As we got off the elevator in the downstairs lobby, our supervisor looked at me and pointed to several newspaper stands about fifty feet away.

"Mr. Blackburn, do I need to go over there with you, or can I trust you from here to do that safely by yourself?"

I looked blankly at her. "You can trust me just to go get the paper. I'm not interested today in running away."

Opening the newspaper as fast as I could, I breathed a sigh of relief that nothing was on the top half of the front page. But there it was, just under the fold, complete with a picture taken of me when I was named Tarheel of the Week. The story was straightforward. It told of the state bar filing and noted that I was now at Duke University Medical Center for an undetermined stay for treatment in the psychiatric wing.

Even though the story was factual, it was another step on the road to disgrace. I understood now why everyone wanted me in the hospital. As much as the story might upset me, there was nothing I could do about it from here, and I wouldn't have to answer any questions.

I found that I had no energy. I had no desire to do anything. I just wanted to lie on my bed and either close my eyes or look at the ceiling. I could not read a book. I did not want to talk to any doctors. I didn't even have the energy to want to die. That would have been too hard. I just wanted to be. And absolutely nothing else.

Late that afternoon, the first of the week's visitors showed up. I wasn't expecting anyone, and when Alan Head, the Executive Director of the State Bar Association, walked in, I was surprised. Alan and I had been classmates at Wake Forest University many years before, and his decision to visit touched me deeply.

By nightfall, Marsha and Stacy appeared at the door, bearing brownies baked by one of our friends.

"Well, Dad, you're big news in Raleigh."

"Yeah, I've read the paper. It wasn't too bad."

"Oh, I'm not talking about the newspaper. That's nothing. It's been on the radio and television all day. Some of my friends had even heard about it before they came to school. And food. Everybody's bringing us food. Mom won't have to cook for a week."

Marsha added, "If that's the worst of it, we can probably live with that."

"Oh, Dad, I brought you someone to stay with you. Miss Molly has decided you need her right now more than I do. But I have to tell you, I've never been without her since I first got her, so you had better take good care of her."

Miss Molly was a small brown bear that Stacy slept with every night and still does to this day. This was no small gift from a fourteen-year-old daughter.

As the week passed my mood lifted somewhat, and I was able to read a book, talk to my doctors, talk to my family on the telephone, and have some contact with the outside world. I asked Rick if he would consider sending a helicopter relief squad over to the hospital to take me away, and he assured me he would. I had every medical test I could imagine. My heart and brain were scanned; the latter showed evidence of a small stroke that likely had been caused by stress sometime in the past. The lab did extensive blood tests that measured certain chemical levels, which, in turn, indicated my level of depression. Doctors questioned me to test my mental faculties.

Everyone close to me was still concerned about my health. They knew another large newspaper story was coming on Sunday and wanted to be sure I could handle it. Jean Spaulding told them I could as long as I was at Duke. Then the questions turned to my release date and where I should go at that time. Jean's main concern was that I go someplace where I could be quiet and undisturbed.

Before that time came, one last blowup occurred. It happened on Saturday morning, when Rick and Marsha discussed Sunday's upcoming newspaper story. The paper planned to reveal everything, including the taking of money. While I had told Marsha about this, neither of our children knew. Jean had advised that Jeff and Stacy should hear only what was necessary. Now, before Sunday's paper came out, they needed to hear it all.

Afterwards, Marsha came to see me alone that afternoon. As she walked into my room, she held up her pocketbook and told me no one checked to see what was in it.

"Why is that important?" I asked.

"Because I could have a gun in here and kill you and then myself and all of this would be over. That's why."

"You're not doing well today, are you, Marsha?"

"No, I'm not. Do you know there are no bridges between our house and this hospital?"

"Why is that important?"

"Because there is nothing to run into or off of, that's why. Jim, this is so awful. People have no idea. I never knew a person could hurt so much and still be alive.

"And there's one more thing. How can you just sit there on that bed and look normal with everything that has happened? My God, when people come to see you, they don't think anything's wrong with you because you smile and talk with them so normally. You even get up and get them a chair and make sure they're comfortable. This is insane."

"Marsha, I'm doing the best that I can. I don't know any other way to act. That's just how I am."

I think back to these comments often and realize they sum up for many people the fall into depression or mental illness, the fall into disgrace, the loss of a job or a loved one. They are feelings that almost everyone goes through at some time. They're part of being human. But, I have learned, it is in hurting that we are healed. We must know despair before we can know true grace.

I lived a long time before I realized that. I hate to think that I had to make such a severe fall to learn that prayer is so good, that close friends and family are so necessary, and that despite what most people say, "God only puts a comma, where too many of us put a period."

I was released from Duke University Medical Center on Monday, exactly one week after I had been admitted. Marsha and I drove straight to Jean Spaulding's office. We discussed where I should go.

"I'm concerned about your going home to Raleigh," Dr. Spaulding told me. "You need absolute quiet and rest. You are very ill, even though you may not know it or agree with it yet. While your stay at Duke gave you some rest and protected you, and we were able to conduct a number of medical tests on you, you were not very helpful to the nurses and doctors. You didn't communicate much. They can't help you if you don't talk to them.

"Now, you are going to have to talk to me, probably much more than you want. I want you here every day this week. Every day," she emphasized. "I want to give you more tests. I want to monitor your medication, and I want to talk to you at great length. You are not out of the woods medically. The slightest interruption could send you over the deep end.

"Finally, you have to be close by where I can see you on a moment's notice. That means either being here in Durham or Raleigh, with the understanding that you must come here at once if anything unusual happens. You must stay inside. You should not talk to anyone but your family and me. No one else. You can't answer the telephone, answer the door, or go anywhere in the car."

"Can I go get the mail from the mailbox?"

"No, Marsha or Jeff or Stacy can do that. You cannot."

For more than a month, that is what I did, except for one trip to Winston-Salem to visit my mother for two days. But before I went, the local newspaper struck again.

Promise You'll Come Back

On Wednesday morning, the day I was to leave for Winston-Salem and just three days after leaving Duke, I opened the newspaper and quickly glanced through it, looking for any sign of my name. Finding none, I got a cup of coffee and sat down in a blue leather wingback chair in the den to read the local section of the paper.

Below the bottom of the fold on the front page, I read some words that looked like my name and the words "Duke Hospital." I flipped the paper over and saw the headline: "Va. State Police and FBI track Blackburn."

I almost fell out of the chair. Marsha, Jeff, and Stacy were still at home that morning. "Have you-all seen this?" I hollered out. No one had.

"I think I'm going back upstairs and lie down. I really don't feel well. You might want to take a look at the paper."

Marsha picked it up and started reading. Within a few minutes, she came upstairs to the bedroom where I was lying down.

"How are you feeling?"

"Not too good."

"I've called Jean and Wade. Jean says she can change her schedule this morning and see us as soon as we can get there. Wade will call from Raleigh. Do you feel like getting in the car and riding over there?"

"Yeah, I can do that."

The newspaper story quoted sources that said I was now under a Virginia state investigation and federal study as well. It recounted some of what had been printed in the larger Sunday edition, complete with pictures of some of the documents I had signed, and a picture of Lake Gaston. In addition, Rick Gammon was quoted as saying he had "a real concern for Jim's physical health."

At Jean's office, we hooked up to a conference call to Wade Smith's office. "Jim, this is Wade. Rick is here with me. We've read the paper this morning and don't blame you a bit for being upset. We can understand that completely. We are angry about it ourselves."

"Is something going on that I don't know about?" I asked.

Rick answered, "I called Al Koehler [FBI agent] at home this morning just after I learned about this article. He knows nothing about an FBI investigation and doesn't think there's going to be one. He's not sure they have any jurisdiction. He also said to tell you hello, and that he and others are thinking about you."

Marsha spoke up. "Both Jim and I are scared. We don't know what to expect. Is somebody coming to the house to take him away? Are television cameras going to be outside our house? Is he about to be arrested and hauled away? What's happening?"

"I don't think anything like that is going to happen now," Rick answered. "Colon Willoughby [the local district attorney] wouldn't do that. That's the last thing that is going to happen to Jim right now. I'd put money on it."

"I agree," said Wade. "Jim, are you still planning to go to Winston-Salem today?"

Jean answered before I did. "My thoughts are that Jim needs to go as scheduled but to check in with us regularly while he's there. He badly needs to get out of town. I think this only serves to further point out his need for hospitalization, and if more insurance coverage was available, he'd still be there."

"I absolutely agree," Wade replied. "Jim, do you still feel like going?"

"Yes, I think so, if everybody else agrees."

"Marsha, what do you think?"

"I'm still in favor of his going. I don't know that he should drive a car right now, though. His focus isn't good."

Jean spoke up. "I very much agree with Marsha. I think Jim should go, but I don't feel comfortable with him driving."

Marsha responded, "I'll work out the driving arrangements. I can take him halfway, and his mother can pick him up. Then, maybe Jim's father can pick him up halfway on the way back."

I couldn't stand it any longer. My parents had been divorced for some time. "That'll be cute. That's how I'm going to die, in the middle of a fight between those two. They haven't spoken to each other in years."

"Jim, do you think you can handle all of this, including your father and mother meeting? They don't have to talk to each other. It can be like one of those prisoner exchanges where the drivers stand at each end of the bridge and only you walk across."

It was settled. I would be escorted to Winston-Salem and back by family. Before the meeting was over, Jean turned to Marsha and said, "I need to speak to Jim alone for just a minute, if you can wait outside."

Jean closed the door to her office, and it was just the two of us.

"Jim, are you going to be okay at home in Raleigh after you come back from Winston-Salem?"

"Yeah, that will be all right. I've been able to rest there the last two nights. I haven't been outside or seen anyone."

"Jim, there's another thing. Before I let you go anywhere, you need to level with me about how you're feeling. You must tell me the truth. I haven't given you too much medicine at one time because I have been worried about what you would do with it."

"You think I'd take it all at once? Jean, I'm not going to kill myself. Not today, at any rate. I already feel better, though I wasn't in good shape this morning."

"That's precisely what I'm concerned about. What's going to happen next time?"

I smiled just a bit. "You think there's going to be a next time?"

"I want to be prepared."

"Jean, we're only talking two days. I'm going to be in Winston-Salem at my mother's. That's about as harmless as it gets. I'm not going to do anything at her house."

"Can I trust you until I see you on Friday at 1:00 P.M.?"

"You can do that. I'll give you until Friday when I see you," I promised.

She sighed. "Jim Blackburn, you're going to give me more gray hairs than I need or want. See all these. You gave me these in just two weeks."

"I don't see but two."

"That's two too many."

"Ok, I'll see you Friday."

"You promise?"

" I promise."

Mother, I Had to Kill You

My mother picked me up in front of the Holiday Inn just off Interstate 40 in Burlington, about an hour's drive from Raleigh. My mother liked to remain young by reminding everyone that she was born in 1917, the same year as President Kennedy, and look how young he remained.

We were close friends. She had followed my career closely. In the early school years, she was my most vocal critic. On the high school debate team, I often had to give public speeches, and before each one I had to practice to near perfection for an audience of one. She had been proud of my success as a lawyer and, like so many mothers of sons, didn't think there was anything I couldn't do and certainly I could do no wrong. This had not been a happy time for her.

Shortly before noon, we left Burlington and were on our way to Winston-Salem. The traffic wasn't too heavy, and even mother, who was not a fast driver, began to relax.

"Mother, I need to tell you something."

"What's that?"

"Well, it's been in the Raleigh *News and Observer,* I understand, though I haven't actually read it myself. But you're going to find out, and you might as well know from me."

"Know what? I don't understand."

"Well, let me tell you, I had to kill you."

There was a long silence as we drove down the road. Finally, "You had to do what?"

"I had to kill you. It was for a good cause though, I suppose. At least, it seemed like it at the time."

Another long silence. "What was the cause?"

"There was this case. I needed a continuance. I couldn't think of a reason, so I used you. You had a heart attack and died. Sort of sudden, though you had been sick for some time."

"How did you come up with that?"

"I don't know. I remembered you did have that slight heart attack back in 1978. Seemed normal to me, so that's how and why you died. It was in the paper."

"It was in Sunday's paper?"

"Yep."

"That explains it then. Bill [my younger brother, who also lives in Winston-Salem] got a copy of the Raleigh Sunday paper but didn't want me to see it. He said he needed to talk with me first."

"So you haven't seen it?"

"No, not yet."

"I'm sorry I did that. I'd never even thought of doing anything like that before. I don't know what got into me, but I'll confess, it did seem like the thing to do at the time."

After awhile, she smiled. "That's okay. I understand. I'm glad it was for a good cause. Tell me though, did you get the continuance?"

"Oh yeah, I got it."

"Good."

Off the Charts

After I returned from Winston-Salem, I saw Jean Spaulding at least three times a week. She asked me questions about my family, my legal profession, every part of my life. I took tests that measured personality and tests that allowed her to study my thinking process.

Against my judgment, she persuaded me to begin regularly attending group therapy sessions at night, in addition to our one-on-one sessions. I found that I was very reluctant to open up to strangers about what had happened to me, other than the facts of my case. It had been well publicized, so that was no problem. But I did not want to talk, with any degree of seriousness, about my mental condition.

During these days, I began to slowly emerge from my home to take long walks, often in William B. Umstead State Park, which was not far from where I lived. There, I could retreat into the woods, walk along dirt trails, and be away from everyone. I discovered that walking is wonderful therapy.

One cold, rainy afternoon in March, Wade Smith and I agreed to go for a long walk on Loblolly Trail in Umstead. The trail is named for the tall pine trees that grow so abundantly in the park. I arrived first and after a few minutes, Wade drove up. I could see what looked like a large package in the front passenger's seat.

The passenger door opened and out jumped Joe McGinniss,

Three good friends on a hike, *left to right,* Wade Smith, me, and Joe McGinness

whom I'd gotten to know well during the time Joe researched his book, *Fatal Vision.* Joe had flown that day from his home in Massachusetts to Raleigh just to go walking with Wade and me. The three of us walked like what seemed forever, and at the end of the afternoon, with muddy boots and wet clothes, we went to 42nd Street Oyster Bar for a prearranged dinner. It was my first social event out of the house since I entered Duke University Medical Center.

I talked to few people, outside my family, on the specific advice of Jean Spaulding. Perhaps I owed friends and others an explanation of what I had done and what was happening to me, but I was in no condition to do that. Slowly, however, friends who had tried to reach me but could not, were allowed to do so. By mid-March, I was permitted to go outside my house to walk with friends, but I always had to let Jean Spaulding know with whom and where I was going.

The first few months of 1993 were spent surviving, and I didn't try to do more than that. The decision to turn in my law license was hard. In making that decision, it made no difference to me that the bar might ultimately take it anyway. To turn away formally from the one objective of my life was simply very painful.

My sessions with Jean continued as she tried to learn what had happened to me. She got very pointed and personal. Her strategy was straightforward. In her words, she said she wanted to tear someone I knew down at first, and then we would build that person back up. In the process, I would discover the impact that person had on my life

In our sessions Dr. Spaulding would ask me such questions as, What in your life has been in Technicolor and what has been in black and white? When was the last time you were carefree and happy? Really happy? Look at these pictures and tell me what they mean to you.

Jean showed me pictures, most in black and white but a few in color. I mostly saw bloody insects and squashed bugs. I guess I saw my own life that way—crushed, destroyed, and mutilated. Jean took a lot more notes.

She asked me about my childhood, my father and mother. Did I like being a lawyer? Why was it so important to me to be liked? Why did I feel it necessary to please everyone? Had I ever learned to say no? Did I ever get angry? Why was I always smiling? Finally, she wanted me to tell her about Jeffrey MacDonald.

"Did you think, after that case, that you had to win them all?" she asked me.

"It was the best and the worst of all possible cases. If I had lost it, then my life would have been completely different. That case was for me that point in your life where one event can change everything. For half of 1978 and all of 1979, all I did was the Mac-Donald trial. That's how I am identified. That's what everybody always asks about. That's how I judge myself now. When I won or lost other cases, it didn't matter. Either way, I judged myself according to the MacDonald case."

"It sounds as though that case has haunted you."

"It set up an impossible standard. I came to believe that I could fix anything, do anything, because I had won that impossible case. I stretched myself too thin. I wanted to be all things to all people. That case became my identity."

At a therapy session later in the spring, Jean came around from behind her desk, where she usually sat, and settled in a chair directly opposite mine. "Jim," she began quietly, "I have some good news and some bad news."

"What's that?"

"Well, there's no doubt about it. You're off the charts. You are one of the worst cases of depression I have ever seen."

"What?" Numb, I asked her to expand on her comments.

"Jim, you have all the classic symptoms of major depression." She began quoting descriptions of these symptoms and how they applied to me. "For example, 'a disorder of sleep in the form of insomnia.' You haven't slept well for a long time. You wake up in the middle of the night and just wait for the morning to come.

"'A disorder of appetite.' You've told me yourself how much weight you have continued to gain over at least the last year.

"'A disorder in the interest in pleasure derived from life in general, consisting of feeling no pleasure whatsoever from either daily activities or extraordinary opportunities.' Jim, all you did when you got home was lay down and wait until it was time to go to sleep. That is all you did. You haven't had any fun or pleasure in so long, you wouldn't know it if it hit you in the face.

"'A disorder of movement consisting of a lack of motoric behaviors that can result in no movement at all or can result in hyperactive movements during a manic phase.' Jim, you may not be manic, but you have been close. You can't sit still. You are always moving. At work, you had difficulty completing tasks because you couldn't stay focused for any length of time.

"'A disorder of mood that can result in complete sadness to the point of a desire for suicide, or during a manic phase can result in marked and abnormal elevation of mood for no apparent reason.' Remember all the mood swings you have had for so long. You are expansive one moment, buying drinks for everybody at the Oyster Bar and being the life of the party, and shortly after you're staring out your office window at work, not able or wanting to finish writing a letter, or just laying on the sofa at home, staring into space.

"'A disorder of thinking whereby one's thought processes may be so slowed that one can hardly speak, or may be so accelerated that one's speech cannot keep pace with one's thoughts, resulting in thought blocking.' You of all people should realize you talk too fast . . . constantly. It is hard for anyone else to speak. Your thoughts race from one topic to another.

"And Jim, while you're not psychotic, you have such symptoms. That land case, writing of those fictitious court orders, flicking that switch on and off in your brain, and talking strategy with clients on a case that did not really exist are all examples.

"You, Jim, are and have been quite depressed."

"I see. Is this the good news or the bad news?"

"Well, I suppose it's good for your case because it demonstrates that you have been and are very sick, and it gives some explanation for your actions. On the other hand Jim, you are really sick. This is no joke."

"I see. What else?"

"My diagnosis is this: You've had a walking-around nervous breakdown. You have a major depressive disorder with what I would call psychotic features. You're not psychotic, but you have had certain features of that in the past. Basically, you have had a break with reality."

"When do you think all this began?"

"We don't know for sure. But it certainly began well in the past. It's not something that occurred this year for the first time, if that's what you mean."

"I guess my lawyers will be pleased. Now, they've got something to say. But I must tell you that I think this makes me feel worse."

"That's completely understandable."

But she didn't really understand, and neither did anyone else. I had been the one most reluctant to go to Duke Hospital, the one most reluctant to see Jean Spaulding in the first place. Now, I was being told how sick I was. I did not like what she told me. I had no idea then what would be done with this information. I only knew that I was not happy. I felt very alone.

I was right about my lawyers' reaction to this news. Wade Smith's first reaction was that we had to release this information to the public, have a press conference with Jean Spaulding present to give her views. Ultimately we did release her diagnosis through an interview that Wade and Rick Gammon had with two reporters of the local paper. In short, we opened up the story of my life for anyone to read.

I spent the remainder of the spring doing little except meet with Jean Spaulding and walk with my family, friends, or by myself. During this time I was aware of an ongoing criminal investigation by the State Bureau of Investigation, but I didn't know much about it, and I did not know what their conclusions would be. My lawyers thought we should make as little noise as possible and hope that it would all go away.

But it was not going away. It couldn't. I was reminded of that every day. I felt like I was living life in a bubble. I existed inside the house, and I could see people living their lives just as they had before. They were busy going to work, to church, to see friends, out to a movie, the normal things that people do. But I wasn't doing any of that. I couldn't.

It was not that I was unable physically to do those things. I learned that spring of the misunderstanding so many people have of mental illness. I was told I should not go to church because I looked too normal to be mentally ill, and the district attorney, who went to the same church, would think I was normal. I was told never to go downtown because I looked healthy.

A friend of mine, meaning well, told me that recently I'd made a mistake. I'd lunched with another friend and he'd heard that I looked as though I was enjoying myself. Bad idea. I should not do that again.

Rick told me the only way I should ever go downtown was in a wheelchair, wearing a bathrobe, and unshaven with several days' growth. Or if I went to church, I should stand up in the middle of the sermon and start shouting and have Marsha pop some pills in me and shove me back down into the pew.

I became increasingly frustrated with everyone. I became angry. A lot of people wanted to help, but no one knew what to do with me or my situation.

I think that today we have come a long way in our understanding of mental illness and the insidious nature of clinical depression. It invades your mind without your knowledge. It can take hold of you and not let you go. It can wreck your life. But you can also beat it. You can recover from it. It does not have to end your life or permanently destroy you or your family. But coming back is hard, very hard.

The hardest thing is accepting that you are in fact suffering from depression. It is not a sexy illness, if there is any such thing. It conjures up impressions of weakness and tiredness. There are no broken bones, only a wounded brain, and no one can see that from the outside.

Still, you must persevere. You cannot give up. You must surrender yourself to those who know more than you do about mental illness. Do not pay much attention to those who question whether anything is wrong with you. They are usually not doctors and have no understanding of mental illness.

One of the first questions I had been asked in early 1993, when all the news about me broke, was whether I would continue to live in Raleigh or leave and try to start over somewhere else. For my family and me, running away was never an option.

Marsha taught special education in high school, and she didn't miss a class. Jeff and Stacy were in school, and they never missed a class. Not one. They faced people every day, and in that way showed far more courage than I had to.

One of my friends told Marsha, "What we need is for the doctors to find a tumor in Jim's brain, cut it out and put it in a jar, so people can see it. That's what we need. No one will ever accept anything else."

Maybe so. What we really needed was for the truth—whatever that was—to be found and used to heal me so that I could be worth something in the future. I am reminded of what I used to tell juries about truth. It comes, if at all, screaming and yelling into the courtroom. It does not come quietly, and it does not come easily. One wages a constant fight for truth.

I remember a poignant interchange I had with Jean Spaulding during one visit. She looked me straight in the eye and said, "You know, Jim, most people don't see the real you. They see some happy, smiling person who acts as though he doesn't have a care in the world, that everything's great."

"I know, I do that pretty well," I acknowledged. "I'll tell you what I am. I'm a great actor, that's what I do best. Sometimes, I can even fool myself. If I show people I'm happy, they don't get too close and ask too many questions. I only let them see what I want them to see, and I don't want people to see that I'm hurting or down. I do comedy well. I don't do tragedy well."

Jean concluded, "But if you combine that part of your personality with your tendency to escape, as you have done, plus a severe depression, you have all the necessary ingredients for an explosion. Which is what you did, explode."

Bad Storm Coming

When bad news is coming as a result of your actions, you survive best if you hunker down and let the big wave wash over you. You might get your head wet and you might eat some sand, but eventually the wave will pass, and if you are strong enough, you will still be safe, with your head above water.

The next big wave was coming for me in the summer of 1993. The criminal investigation of my conduct was ending. They had one last witness to interview, me. I met with two agents of the State Bureau of Investigation (SBI) in Rick's conference room for a conversation that lasted hours. My lawyers' advice was direct and simple: tell everything and tell it truthfully. I did. I answered every question they put to me and held nothing back. They could have written an indictment that afternoon based solely on what I gave them.

That afternoon was one of the first milestones on my road back. I told the truth. I confronted the evidence. I did not rely on a defense of any kind. I did not run away.

Later, on Friday, July 9, 1993, I had lunch with an old friend, Kim Dupree, who had once worked for me when I had my own law office in the mid-1980s. Kim was a recent graduate of Meredith College in Raleigh. She's very pretty with long dark hair. She had been a flight attendant with Delta Airlines and seen the world. On many of her travels, she had often sent me postcards telling me she was reading about Jeffrey MacDonald in the book *Fatal Vision*.

She asked me gently what was going on in my case, and whether I thought District Attorney Colon Willoughby would bring criminal charges against me. I told her I didn't know. All I knew was that the SBI had interviewed me and I thought the investigation was probably over. So far, everything was quiet. I was hopeful nothing would happen.

Later that afternoon, shortly after five o'clock, I settled down in the basement room of our house with a glass of wine, looking forward to the weekend. I sat in an easy chair by the fireplace with my laptop computer. I was working on a novel involving a well-known attorney in Raleigh who was under suspicion for the murder of his brother and law partner. I was making it up as I went along and had written almost two hundred pages. I sat there, waiting for inspiration to strike. Instead the telephone rang.

"Jim, this is Wade. I've got Rick on the other line. Are you there, Rick?"

"Yes, I'm here. Hello, Jim."

Wade continued. "We talked to Colon today. He's read the SBI report, and said he was very troubled by it." He paused, "Jim, there's another storm coming. You're going to have to put down all your anchors, be strong, and hold on tight. You can get through this, but it will take enormous courage, more than you've had to have so far. I want to tell you this will be *hard*."

"Are you telling me the DA's decided to indict me?"

"He didn't say that, he never said that. In fact, he said he was going to read the report again this weekend. But I think we have got to prepare for the worst."

"Do you know when this is going to be? Monday?"

"No, I don't think it will be Monday, but soon."

"Do you think it will be Tuesday?"

"It could be."

"Rick, what do you think? Do you agree with Wade?"

"Yes, I do."

Wade spoke again. "There are a number of things we think you should do and do quickly. First, you're going to have to recognize that your life is going to change. I mean immediately. You're going to have to sell your house and move to some other place. You can't stay in that house, it's too nice. You don't need that much space anyway. You need a For Sale sign in your yard next week. People need to see that you're suffering, that you're being hurt. That will help you.

"You've got to sell your car, you can't keep riding around in that BMW convertible, even if it is old. It's simply too nice and stands for money and all the wrong things. People see you riding around in that car, and they won't think you've been hurt at all, that everything's the same. Business as usual. You need to walk, take a bus, get a ride with somebody, or be seen in the worst car you can find. Jim, you have got to be humbled. Otherwise, you are not going to survive. You will go down forever.

"You need to get rid of as many things as you can. You should begin to take these steps now. Next week is not too soon. You need to raise money yourself to pay back the firm. You can't borrow the money—it has to come from you."

He continued listing changes I needed to make.

"What is the Wake Forest President's Club? You've got to get out of that."

"Wade, I've told you before, that's just a level of financial giving to Wake Forest. There's nothing to get out of, except giving them money. I don't get anything in return."

"I know, but it sounds bad. You've got to get out of it. Jim, perception is everything. If it were named something other than the President's Club, it would be okay."

"You've got to resign from everything and give up any of the clubs to which you belong. Which clubs do you belong to?"

"The City Club and the Cardinal Club."

"Resign on Monday. Get out of them. They cost money, and it doesn't look good. You can't go eat there now anyway."

"And, of course, there is the country club."

On this they yelled in unison.

"Jim, you absolutely have to give that up. You cannot be seen going there. That place is a symbol to many people."

"What else?"

"You can't teach Sunday School any more. You shouldn't be seen at church. Jim, we know you've been sick. But the public doesn't understand mental illness. You look normal. People don't understand that. You have to be bandaged up, in a wheelchair, or dying in a hospital for anyone to believe you're sick. Going to church is normal. Teaching makes you look like nothing is wrong.

"One more thing. You've got to realize you're going to be poor for some time to come. Marsha is going to have to realize that also. You can't buy anything. Both of you are going to have to make extreme sacrifices."

"Why should I sell my house?"

"Jim, you've got to do that. You're not going to be able to make the payments. If you go to prison, Marsha won't be able to keep up the house on her own, and she won't need that big a house anyway."

"How do you know I won't be able to make the payments? I have so far."

"Jim, you need to look at this, what you're facing."

"Wade, what do you think the chances are of my getting a substantial sentence?"

"About fifty-fifty."

I took a moment to absorb this.

Wade continued, "Jim, listen, you can come through this. What it's going to take is absolutely enormous courage, as much as you have. If you will put your head down and survive this, go to the bottom and let this wave wash over you, then you can be free of this and begin to come back. The truth is you need for this moment to come. You need to have one great cathartic moment for this to all come out. If you don't, it will follow you and haunt you for the rest of your life."

"I understand. What happens now?"

"I'm getting ready to go to my place on the river for the weekend," Wade answered. "But I'll be thinking about you this weekend and what we can do. We'll need to meet first thing on Monday. I'll call you tomorrow. I'll be around."

Rick spoke, "I'm going to be out of town this weekend, too, but I'll check in with you."

Wade continued, "Jim, we're going to meet with the district attorney on Monday morning. Maybe there's a chance he won't indict, that nothing will happen. He didn't say he definitely would, just that he was bothered by the report. But if he's made up his mind, nothing will change him. That's why you have to prepare yourself this weekend. Are you okay?"

"Yeah, I'm okay. See you guys."

"We'll talk to you soon."

The telephone call had taken less than fifteen minutes. Slowly, I took the laptop computer from the ottoman in front of my chair and placed it on the floor beside me. I walked across the room and replaced the portable telephone on its receiver and returned to my chair. After turning off the lamp beside me, I leaned back and closed my eyes.

I tried to think of a way out of this mess. I went through everything Wade and Rick said, and I thought of every available option that could prevent an indictment. But as the minutes went by and the tears began to well in my eyes, I slowly acknowledged, if not accepted, the awful truth that there was no way out.

A few minutes later, I heard Marsha call and say that supper was ready. I picked myself up and walked up the stairs to the table near the kitchen. Marsha and Stacy, our fourteen-year-old daughter, were already eating spaghetti, and mine was getting cold.

One look at me and my eyes told them something was wrong. I didn't hold back. I told them about my talk with Wade and Rick. They listened quietly and didn't ask any questions. Marsha put her right hand on my left hand. Stacy told me she loved me and began to tear up as well. Somehow, we managed to eat supper.

I got up from the table and went back downstairs and sat alone in the dark. I felt there was no way out. There was nothing I could do. For the first time in my life, I could not make it better.

I remembered my attorneys' saying I would be poor and that our family would just have to get used to it. Sitting there in the dark, I rebelled at that thought. It was one thing for me to go straight to hell; it was another to take every one else with me.

I thought some more. How could I get money for my family? How could I prevent them from being poor? How could I prove Wade and Rick wrong? Finally, the idea came to me, as it does to almost anyone who is desperate and not thinking clearly. By taking my own life, I could guarantee a large sum of insurance money to Marsha, Jeff, and Stacy.

I began to feel better, relaxed even. If someone had seen or spoken to me at that time, I would have appeared totally at ease. My life, as I had always known it, was over. There was no reason to save it any longer. Carefully, I went over every person in my family and easily concluded that each would be better off without me, or at least have more money.

Everything turned black. I felt boxed into a corner with only one way out.

I felt very lonely. That night there was no one else for me. There was no family, no friends, no God, no anyone or anything that I now wanted except to end it all and not suffer any longer. I wanted out.

All of us go through life feeling lonely at times. We all experience disappointment, heartache, great sadness, and many of us think for a fleeting moment about escaping life. Gladly, most of these thoughts pass with no real harm done. That happened to me.

I decided to go away later that night and drive hundreds of miles to Hilton Head Island, South Carolina, where our family had gone to the beaches for years. I loved Hilton Head. Some of the happiest weeks of past summers had been spent there. I had given my kids bike rides all over the island, walked on the wide sandy beaches, and swam in the warm calm waters. If I were to die, this is where I would choose to do it.

At about 8:00 P.M., I walked upstairs to get my car keys and leave. Marsha and Stacy were upstairs. Stacy saw me first.

"Dad, what are you doing? Are you feeling any better?"

"Not really. I may go out for awhile."

"Where are you going? Do you want me to go with you?"

"Well, if you must know, I am thinking of driving to the beach. To Hilton Head."

"Now, you're going where? And what are you going to do when you get there?"

"I thought I might go for a swim."

"Dad, let me tell you something. I have been really supportive of you this year. So have Jeff and Mom. But if you decide to do something stupid, I will really be mad at you. I will not forgive you for doing that to us. Not after all this."

"Now, look, Stacy. Both Wade and Rick said we are going to be poor this way. Well, the way I see it, that doesn't have to happen. I've got a lot of life insurance on me. If I die, the family is okay."

"Dad, that is really dumb. The money is not important. We love you."

"Stacy, it's a lot of money."

"That doesn't make any difference."

"A real lot of money."

"Okay, Dad, how much money?"

"Six hundred thousand dollars."

SILENCE.

One way out. I considered driving to my favorite beach spot, Hilton Head Island, for a final swim

"Dad, you know, I have to tell you . . . that is a lot of money. We may actually want to think about this."

"What!"

She started laughing. "I'm just kidding, Dad."

Slowly, I started to laugh as well. Marsha, who had been listening to all this from inside the bedroom, joined us and motioned for me to sit down on the bed. Stacy stood in the doorway. Time passed, and as it did, the thoughts of selfishness and despair and hopelessness faded away.

As I sat there on the bed, I realized for the first time the twin powers of laughter and unconditional love. Both had combined that night to give me another chance. They had bought me time.

Hope is the single ingredient needed to prevent the taking of one's life. *But hope is not possible without adequate time to find it.* That is often the difference between life and death.

I spent the remainder of the evening in pursuing just that. I called an old friend, the chief State Bureau of Investigation agent, Bill Dowdy. Bill had been with the SBI most of his career and was known to law enforcement and defense attorneys alike as a tough, but straight, shooter. He was both that night for me. Bill is big and tough, and bears more than a passing resemblance to the television cop, Kojak. Bill is honest, completely ethical, and a good friend.

"Bill, is that you?"

"Hello, boy. How are you?"

"Well, I've been better. Wade and Rick told me tonight that I am going to be indicted."

"Yes, I know. I talked to Colon Willoughby several days ago. He doesn't like this at all, but he's got to do his job."

"I understand that. That's what he should do. Bill, do you think I can survive this?"

"Absolutely. The worst is behind you—that was back in January. You do what you have to do, and sure, you can come back from this."

"What do you think Colon is going to do at sentencing?"

"I think he'll ask for active time. He thinks that's what he has to do."

"You know, Bill, when this is all over, I sure would like to have lunch with you again. I've missed that this year."

"Hell, we can go now."

"You mean that?"

"Absolutely. Give me a call next week, and we can set it up."

"Tell you what. I'll wait until after the indictment and then call you. I'll need a good lunch by then."

I lay back on the bed and looked at the ceiling, trying to relax and not think. Sometimes, not thinking is the best thinking of all.

Close to 11:00 P.M., the telephone rang. It was Wade.

"Jim, I can't sleep, and I'm sure you can't either. Do you want to meet me somewhere and have a cup of coffee? Where can we go?"

"Any place is okay with me."

"I know, let's meet at IHOP in fifteen minutes."

It was Friday night, and the International House of Pancakes was crowded. We got a booth near the front of the restaurant and ordered coffee and eventually breakfast. As we passed the little time remaining in that night, we talked about the upcoming indictment and how we would handle it. We discussed strategy, but there wasn't much. Mostly, we talked about life.

Wade flipped a place mat over and wrote "Not Guilty" on one side and "Guilty" on the other. He jotted down thoughts and ideas under each heading. Even though his writing was upside down for me, I could tell he was writing more, much more, in the "Guilty" column.

Finally, I could take it no longer and my humor kicked in. Sitting here in a local restaurant at one o'clock in the morning discussing pending felony indictments, not of some unknown client but of myself. I leaned across to Wade and whispered to him, "Wade, you know, being convicted of a felony is a bad thing, but I've always been told it's not bad as an aphrodisiac. What do you think?"

He looked at me and didn't miss a beat. "Jim, there is no doubt. Being indicted and convicted of a felony is one of the great aphrodisiacs in the world. I've been thinking of doing it myself."

We paid our bill and walked outside into the warm night. We stood in the parking lot trying to decide how to say good-bye. Finally, Wade looked pensively at me and asked, "Jim, what do you think you have learned from this? What is the great lesson of life that you can take from here?"

I looked down at the pavement and thought a moment. I felt like I'd gone through a whirlwind during the past several hours.

It was now 1:15 in the morning. I was going to be indicted within seventy-two hours.

I thought of a response and didn't hesitate. "I have learned that the next time I forge somebody's signature, I'm going to do it with my left hand. That's what I think about all this."

He looked stunned. Then he got it. After such a bad night, my sense of humor was all I had left. He laughed out loud. Still chuckling, we got into our cars and drove home.

But there was one more person to face. As I unlocked the side door of my house that led into the hallway off the kitchen, I noticed immediately that lights were still on. As I walked into the kitchen, my son Jeff, fully dressed, came down the stairs from his room. His portable telephone was lying on the counter as if he was waiting for a call. He stood near the refrigerator and I was just a few feet away.

"Mom told me what happened tonight."

"Did she tell you I'm going to be indicted, probably next week?"

"Yes."

Tears began to burn in my eyes. "Jeff, I am very sorry."

"Do you think it is for certain?"

"Yes, I do."

"Dad, no matter what happens, I love you. Nothing can change that."

"I love you too, Jeff."

"I'm going out in a few minutes to talk with some friends."

"That's okay. Will you be around tomorrow?"

"Yes."

"Maybe we can have a long talk then. I'll go over everything so you'll know what's going on and there won't be any surprises."

"That's good. I'd like that."

"I think I'm going to bed. I am really tired."

We put our arms around each other and hugged. I told him good night, walked out of the lighted kitchen into the darkened foyer, and up the stairs to bed. As I reached the top of the stairs, I heard his phone ring and then the sound of muffled voices. A couple of minutes later, as I got ready to lie down on the bed, I heard the door close and the sound of a car engine. He was gone.

Back in January, a former law partner of mine had written me a note that read in part, "Each of us, at some time, has to go through our own private Gethsemane. It is a part of being human." At that time, I did not understand what he meant. But as the year passed, this note stood out in my mind as the most precious one of all that I had received. Now would come my test. Earlier in the evening, I had almost failed. I still didn't know whether I would succeed, but I decided to try.

But that would have to wait until tomorrow. Tonight, too much had happened, and I fell asleep as soundly as I ever had. You would not have thought I had a care in the world.

Indictment

That weekend, my mind raced totally out of control. I wrote letters of apology and explanation to members of the law firm. I organized yard sales to raise money to pay the law firm back. I tried to sell off Oriental rugs, silver service sets, cameras, bikes, anything and everything that I no longer needed, wanted, or could use. I was frantic to get my honor back, and I hoped to partially accomplish that by setting things right with the firm. For about two hours, I considered chucking it all and going into the ministry. My father's reaction to that was, "Slow down!" My SBI buddy Bill Dowdy just wanted to know if I had lost my mind.

On Monday shortly before the indictment, I met with Wade and Rick at Wade's office to discuss case strategy, which is really a fancy way of saying, "What the hell do we do now?" Bill Dowdy had suggested to me several ways that I could ease my pain, such as waiving indictment and pleading guilty to a presentment, which was simply a charge by the district attorney that might spare me the grand jury action and one more day of bad news stories. I mentioned this idea to Wade and Rick. They were not impressed.

At the end of the meeting, as I was getting ready to leave, Wade walked over to me and slapped me hard on my shoulder. I fell back in my chair, shocked.

Left, Attorney Rick Gammon and I enter the courtroom for a hearing on charges I'd faked court documents and misused clients' money

"Why did you do that?"

"Jim, you have got to stand tall and face this thing head on. Let Colon indict you. Let them arrest you. Put up your house for security. Don't let them give you any special breaks because of who you are. Look them in the eye and tell them the truth.

"The public will either nail you now or nail you later. This is your defining moment, Jim. If you handle it well, the public will respect you. Tell the truth and take your punishment. It's the way to win, the only way."

I looked back at Wade, stunned. Rick was quiet, except to say that he agreed with Wade.

I lowered my head. For the first time in front of either of them, I became teary eyed. I sat there for a long moment.

Finally, I looked up and said, "All right. I'll do that. I would like for somebody someday to know that I was willing to do this and ask for no favors of any kind."

"Jim, if you get a break, I fear you'll never get well. Nor will it be easy to come back into the work world. But if you take your punishment without asking for special consideration, you'll be healthier, and it's the quickest way to achieve forgiveness from the people around you and from the public. Do this and you'll come back to greater rewards than you ever knew."

The next day the indictment came. I had lived much of my professional life around criminal indictments. I had written them in the United States Attorney's office and had later challenged them while defending my clients as a defense attorney. An indictment is really only a paper, typed by a government secretary from a form given by the prosecutor. Often it's a fill-in-the-blank document. It represents a charge—not evidence or proof—that a crime has been committed, and says that the person named in the indictment is responsible for that crime. That's it.

A trial judge will often tell a jury at the beginning of a criminal trial: The government must prove its case. Everyone is presumed innocent. Make no presumption against an individual based solely on the fact that a person has been indicted.

Now, let me give you the reality of being on the receiving end. An indictment is a damning, horrible thing to happen to you. It is a public document, agreed upon by a group of citizens, that charges you with violating the criminal law. It can cause you to be arrested. It can cause you to have to post bond. It requires that a date be set so that a trial by your peers can determine your guilt or innocence.

I must say here, I was not an easy client to represent. In fact, I was downright difficult. I was angry, paranoid, scared, and embarrassed.

I had also been unemployed since mid-January. I needed a job. Everybody said so. Jobs for ex-lawyers under pending indictment do not abound, however. If convicted on all twelve counts,

I could receive a maximum of 110 years in prison. Not many employers were knocking on my door.

So I knocked on one. I went to the 42nd Street Oyster Bar and talked to Brad Hurley, the manager and part-owner. Brad was a middle-aged man, balding more than he wanted, smoking more than he should, and liking nothing better than to play golf, tell a good joke, and make money. He was good at all three.

"Brad, I need a favor."

"Sure, man, what can I do? You need a job?"

"As a matter of fact, I do."

"Are you serious? I was just kidding with you."

"No, I need a job. Sort of a different job from what I used to do. I want one where I'm in the back somewhere. I don't want to wear a coat or tie. I don't want to be seen. I'll do anything. I'll wash dishes, sweep the floor, you name it."

"Do you want to work here?"

"No, I don't think I should. It's too hot and public, you know?"

"Yeah, I see what you mean. But I don't think you want to wash dishes. I mean, Jesus Christ."

"But, Brad, I've got to do something, and it's got to be something totally different from practicing law."

"Can you cook?"

"Not really," I laughed. "You want me to cook?"

"Well, not here, but you could cook over at the Border Cafe. We own part of that too, and I could speak to my partner, John Vick, over there."

"But what if I really don't know how to cook?"

"Don't worry about it. They can teach you all you need to know. They go by a book."

"It better be a good book."

Brad laughed. "Come see me in about a week. I'll see what I can do."

And so began my career as a cook at the Border Cafe.

The Border Cafe was a tex-mex restaurant in north Raleigh,

decorated in a southwestern motif. The front page of the menu referred to the food as "Fresh From the Great Southwest."

The waiters and waitresses were young people either in or just out of college. They were cheery and happy, and wore the Border's uniform of beige slacks and purple shirts.

The cooking and dishwashing staff was different. Some were older. One had recently arrived from Africa and was studying for a time in the United States. He worked this job and at least one other to make enough money to survive. Most had prior restaurant experience, maybe even cooking. Not me. I was the rookie. We wore black pants, white shirt, a white apron, and a blue baseball hat that had the name and emblem of the Border Cafe stenciled on it.

On my first night I was told, "Hey, Jim, how about going back to the dishwashing area and bringing up some dinner plates. We're about out, and we need to get ahead for the night. You can put them in the warmer there."

I did as I was told and with a large number of white dinner plates in my hands I started back toward the kitchen. Nobody told me that when you wash dishes, you get soap and water on the floor, and water on a tile floor becomes very slippery. I fell on my ass. The back of my head hit the floor with a thud.

Immediately, the two dishwashers rushed to my side to see if I was all right. I was, and they helped me up. Although somewhat embarrassed, I'd passed a major test—I hadn't broken a single dish. They all landed on my chest.

"Jim, maybe you ought to come up here and cut up some chicken."

"Sure, yeah, I can do that." I cut chicken into little pieces for the next two hours. When I left that night, I was as tired as I had ever been in my life.

My next lesson in humility occurred a few days later. It was about lunchtime on a very hot and humid August afternoon, and I didn't have a car that day. I was scheduled to work at the restaurant, which was about six miles from my house, at 4:00 P.M.

I didn't think about asking for a ride. I decided to ride my bike, carrying my work uniform in a plastic bag that hung down from the handlebars. I didn't realize how hilly Raleigh was until that afternoon. After riding about three miles, I stopped at a service station, parked my bike, scooped ice out of the ice bin, and held it against my face.

About two miles later, I hit a bump on a sidewalk and went tumbling over the front of the bike, tearing my bag of clothes. I got up and found them scattered in someone's front yard. I gathered them and tried to get started again. Nothing happened. The fall had broken the bike chain, and that bike was moving only if I pushed it.

About that time, I realized I had become overheated. I promptly threw up. Just as I finished that, I saw a friend I'd once taught Sunday school with, pulling to a stop. She was driving her new Lexus.

She called out, "Jim, are you okay? Do you need a lift, or do you want to put your bike in the trunk of my car?"

"Hey, Harriet. Thanks, but I don't think so. I'll be all right. But you could do something for me. You may not know this, but I'm now cooking at the Border Cafe just down the street. Could you please go by there and tell them I'll be a little late, but that I will get there?"

"Sure, but is that enough? Isn't there something else I can do?"

"No, that'll help a lot. Thanks."

Harriet drove off and I started pushing my bike. A few minutes later, the sky turned dark and heavy rain began to fall. I found a large fir tree near the entrance to an apartment complex, ditched my broken bike, and huddled under the tree to stay dry.

After about twenty minutes the rain eased up, and I started walking toward the restaurant. About a hundred yards away, I saw Sheila driving by and laughing. I demanded to know what was so funny while I threw my bike into the back and rode with her the remaining yards to work.

At the restaurant, I walked into the cooler, found the coldest cloth I could, drowned it with water, and slapped it on my face. I stayed in there until I started to cool off. Next I found a water pitcher, filled it, and drank it all. Finally, I thought I might live.

After working an eight-hour shift that night, I told Marsha I believed I was carrying my guilt complex a little too far. Next time I'd ride in a car.

I stayed at the Border Cafe for six weeks. During that time, I learned how to prepare such favorites as quesadillas, burritos, buffalo wings, nachos, Border fries, taco salads, Caesar salads, and salsa. I learned how to throw hot baked potatoes down the line, over the heads of the others, so they could be put on plates.

I learned that you warm up orders by putting the food itself back on the grill, not the plate, a lesson that caused much merriment among the wait staff.

I learned to endure eight straight hours of rap music, and I almost learned to understand the language the rest of the cooking staff used.

I learned how to close down the kitchen, to clean up, to hose everything down at one o'clock in the morning.

Most of all, I learned that there is no such thing as a menial job. I was not too good to do what I was doing.

I stopped working there at the insistence of my doctor and lawyers. While the indictment was pending, I went overboard in my zeal to work, go to therapy sessions, help start a depression group, volunteer at Food Shuttle, go to Bible Study Fellowship meetings, and do anything else that might help me reclaim my soul and honor.

Another doctor was appointed by the Superior Court, at the request of the district attorney, to determine whether I was competent to proceed with the case. After much discussion and many private meetings, Dr. Seymour Halleck, a well-known and respected forensic psychiatrist at the University of North Carolina at Chapel Hill, determined in the late fall of 1993 that I was competent to go forward.

Dr. Halleck agreed with Dr. Spaulding's conclusions that I was suffering from severe depression, bordering on mania. He added the opinion that I had a severe personality disorder, which could be considered crippling in that I attempted to please too much and went to great excess so that people would like me.

I listened to all these conclusions with a degree of detachment. That was the only way I could accept what was being said. I didn't like it, but at some level, I had decided to surrender and accept whatever conclusion was reached.

That decision took a great deal of trust on my part. Surrendering yourself, even in a mental framework, is not easy. You place the future of your mental wellbeing totally in the hands of someone else. Basically, you give up fighting others' recommendations about your health. That is what I did.

When you've been charged with serious crimes and you have two of the best attorneys to represent you, you would think that great effort would be spent on building a potential legal defense to the charges against you. That was not entirely true in my case. The problem was that I was guilty of the crimes charged in the indictment, and the main issue for me was to survive as a human being with some quality of life left.

I remember the early days of my case when Wade told everyone he saw, "Pray for a miracle." I remember the telephone conversation we had in which he told me, "They can't give you the death penalty, so you will live through this." I remember both Rick and Wade telling me I could handle all of this as long as I was courageous and just held on.

Those are easy words to say. They are not easy to do. So Wade Smith, the grandson of a Baptist minister, and I, the son and grandson of Baptist ministers, went to the Scriptures. He told me repeatedly to read the Sermon on the Mount in the book of Matthew in the New Testament.

I must have read it dozens of times. The essence of what Wade and Rick tried to instill in me was that I had to take whatever was coming. I had to face reality and hold my head up. I could not take the easy way out on anything. If someone wanted me to walk one mile, I should walk two. I was told to turn the other cheek to people who might wish to harm me. I was told to be humble and to pray in private.

They told me to be the very best that I could be.

That was the advice my lawyers gave me for an entire year. It was not based on reading the SBI report, the interviews of any witnesses, the legal research of any cases, or the briefing of any of the finer points of law. It was based on what I had to do to survive. Live the truth as fully as possible.

Thinking back to that time, I am embarrassed that it took so much persuasion to convince me to do the right thing. I should have done it on my own. Many people do so on much graver issues than mine. But at least I finally did it. That is a tribute, I think, to Wade and Rick, to Jean Spaulding, to my family and close friends, all who gently nudged me in the direction that I ultimately went. Of all the things in my life of which I am most proud, taking that last step was one of the best.

Pre-Con Dad

By late November 1993, I had accepted the fact that I was going to plead guilty to all counts of the twelve-count indictment. The district attorney would dismiss no counts and no plea bargain would be negotiated. It would be an open plea. I would plead to the entire indictment with no guarantee of any sentence. The judge would be free to give me whatever sentence he thought I deserved.

In the early fall, I had thought such an idea preposterous. Anyone who willingly did that was certifiably crazy. I had to learn one final lesson. To whom much is given, much is required. I had been given much by the legal profession, and when I fell, I could not be given—nor could I accept—any benefits or special treatment. So when I walked into the Superior Court on the third floor of the Wake County Courthouse on the first Monday after Thanksgiving, I took a deep breath and pleaded guilty to all charges.

It was a sobering experience. Rick had tried to cushion the blow by telling me that there was no real difference between pleading guilty to one felony or one hundred. Wade kept whispering to me, "You're doing the right thing." The fact that Rick and Wade were right did not make it any easier.

Accepting full responsibility for my actions was a step I felt I had to take. I could not blame anyone else, only me. Without this step, redemption would not be possible.

During the week between pleading guilty and being sentenced, I spoke to a group of young women at St. Mary's School in Raleigh. Along with two friends of mine, we spoke to the student body about depression, happiness, and the acceptance of responsibility. It is true that whenever God closes a door, He opens a window.

I must say that I did not particularly want to take whatever the court was going to give me. What I really wanted was for the court to mail me its decision on sentencing. Like every defendant in a criminal case, I also wanted probation; I did not want to go to jail. Sentencing day was Monday, December 6, 1993, almost a full year after I left the law firm.

Sitting in a sentencing hearing when you are the one being sentenced is a wrenching experience. The prosecutor first set out the factual record before the judge, listing precisely all I had done.

Listening to all this were my family and close friends. Everyone was dressed up as though it was Sunday. Everyone was quiet. Everyone was on their best behavior and attentive because no one wanted to influence the judge against me.

Have you ever noticed that when someone is saying something bad about you, it seems to go on forever, and the person never shuts up? It seemed that way to me. I kept wanting to jump out of my chair and run to the witness stand and put tape across the mouth of the SBI witness who was testifying. I wanted the district attorney to lose his voice. I wanted the electrical power to go out . . . something . . . anything . . . I just didn't want to sit there listening to all those accusations.

I think the sentencing hearing itself is part of the punishment that a person receives. First, because you have to listen to the record of events that brought you there, and secondly, the suspense. You have no idea what the judge is going to do with you.

That judge has your life in his or her hands, and don't you think otherwise.

The hearing went on all afternoon. After testimony by the state, my doctors, and arguments by the district attorney for an active sentence and by my attorneys for probation, the judge looked at me and gave me one last chance to speak.

I knew this would happen. I had thought about what I might say. But when it was time, I forgot about what I'd prepared and simply spoke, as best I could, from the heart. I apologized to everyone, in particular the judges across the state and to all the members of the state bar. I also apologized again to my law firm, saying that I was particularly sorry that Dick Ellis had to testify at the sentencing hearing. I recognized publicly that what I did was wrong. I remember saying that I wish Dick were there to hear me say these things. I thought he'd left. Later I learned that he had come back and had lowered his head when I said I wish he were there.

The judge listened attentively and then read from prepared notes as soon as I was through. He was gracious and complimented me on my past life, even telling me he felt I would make a contribution to society once again, sometime in the future. The first sentence he gave me was for a term of three years. The second one was for ten years, and after a long pause, he finally said, "Suspended."

At that point, Wade leaned over to me and said, "So far he hasn't given us anything we can't handle."

I remember thinking, "What's this *we* stuff?"

The judge ordered that I report for prison on the Monday after New Year's to serve the first sentence. Suddenly the hearing was over. My family and friends walked out of the courtroom, down the three flights of stairs, and out into the darkened night to Wade's office for a final word about what it all meant.

I knew that it meant I would go to prison for a short while. Under North Carolina law at that time, a year translated into approximately one month. I was looking at a period of three to four months if all went well. I said to Wade as we went up the street, "If I'd been the prosecutor instead of Colon, I'd have gotten more time. I would have killed me with kindness and disappointment." Wade looked at me in amazement and then nodded that he agreed.

That hearing gave me hope, because the sentence was not forever. I knew I would survive. I would be able to see my children go to school and not miss the rest of their youth. Until that afternoon, that question had remained in doubt.

I'd gotten a miracle after all, although it didn't feel like it at the time. But I needed an active prison sentence; I did not need to escape firm punishment. This was the only way that I could reclaim my life.

Every Christmas and New Year's, I think about this year the most. It is the year I had the most to lose and probably, looking back, the most to gain. Material things became totally unimportant. Freedom and love were all that mattered.

Whenever Marsha or I had to be away overnight or for the weekend, Stacy had a heartwarming habit of writing us a note and leaving it on a pillow or a dresser top. On the day that I left for prison, she wrote me a note and left the card downstairs on the kitchen table so I'd find it after she left for school.

The card read in part:

Daddy,

Hey Pre-con, what's up? As if I actually had to ask. Well I guess this is the last time I can call you Pre-con, now I'll have to just call you plain old con, but that's okay. I'm sure that, as Jeff would say, we can shake it off.

Well, I don't exactly know what to tell you except that you should keep watch out your window for me to break you free. I'm sure I could get some people to help. I'm just kidding, Dad.

Well, I hope everything goes okay this first night. Just know that I will be thinking about you. Hey, remember you have to find time to talk to the trees or, if you can't get out, just talk to your dictaphone.

I'm sorry I can't see you this afternoon before you leave, but of course I have practice. I'll try to score a couple of points for you. I will miss you, but I'll come see you soon, and I'm sure it won't be as long as we think. Don't forget to smile for the cameras!

P.S. I love you Paw—just think about being able to say I'm going to Disney World!

Orange Is Not My Color

The night of January 3, 1994, was the first night I spent in jail. At about 4:00 P.M. that afternoon, Wade, Rick, and I walked the few blocks from Wade's office to the jail lobby, at which time they promptly disappeared. A kindly female deputy sheriff apologetically put handcuffs on me just before I walked through the sliding glass door. The lock snapped shut behind me.

In a long hall immediately in front of me stood deputy sheriffs, dressed in sharply pressed brown uniforms. They confidently and firmly directed men in orange uniforms from room to room, standing them in front of a camera to have their mug shots taken.

During my time as a criminal defense lawyer, I had often seen lines of inmates, linked to each other by locked chains and wearing those orange jumpsuits, waiting to go into court.

As I looked around, numb at being there, I heard a deputy sheriff call my name. She asked me to come over to the counter and answer some basic questions for bookkeeping purposes. As she typed my answers in the computer, she asked my birth date, social security number, and whether I had any sexually transmitted diseases.

"Do I what?"

On January 3, 1994, I tell my attorneys, *left*, Rick Gammon and *right*, Wade Smith good-bye as I report to the Wake Public Safety Center for my first night in jail

She laughed, and repeated her question.

"No, I don't."

I went back to stand against the wall opposite the counter. I waited. For those of you who don't think being locked up for a short time is severe punishment, let me tell you that you are wrong. The big thing about prison is that you are there and you are not free. You cannot move or go anywhere without permission. You have no independence, no control over what you eat, where you sleep, what time you get up, what time you go to bed, and all the time you must wear clothes that the state has given you, and each piece of clothing has a number on it. So "an unfortunate incarceration" for whatever length of time is a big deal. I felt demeaned. I felt powerless. I felt alone.

Just at that moment, I heard another officer call my name again. "Mr. Blackburn, we have someone from the Department of Correction here to interview you for a few minutes. I'm going to have you go upstairs to a small meeting room where we can talk. I know you've just had your handcuffs taken off, but we need to put them on again. It's procedure, whenever you move around the jail. One more thing, we need to take the shoelaces out of your shoes. You'll get them back at some point, but you can't wear them in here."

"I understand. You do whatever you have to."

I don't know why, but giving up my shoelaces and walking around in unlaced shoes proved to be most demeaning. I felt self-conscious, that surely everyone was looking at me and my unlaced shoes. Like an orange jumpsuit, it labeled me a prisoner.

I entered the small conference room one floor above and took a seat behind a large wooden table. I faced the jailer and an officer from the Department of Correction.

"We want to know who you've prosecuted in the past that you think might now be in prison and want to hurt you."

"I can't think of anyone. That was a long time ago, and it was in federal court. The people I convicted went to federal prison."

"What about clients, any of those?"

"No, the only ones are probably on death row."

"Well, that's in a different prison. They're at Central."

The conversation wound down and the correction officer turned to the jailer and asked when I could leave for Troy, North Carolina. Troy is a small town in the middle of the state where a medium-security prison processes all inmates sentenced to anywhere from two to twenty years.

After the officer left the room, the jailer turned to me. "Jim, I want to tell you something that the officer cannot say to you. He is prohibited by regulation from doing so. And if he should ask me if I said anything about it to you, I will absolutely deny it. Understand?"

"I understand. What is it?"

"You do not need to be housed in the general population at Troy. You need to ask now to be placed in protective custody. Believe me, I've seen these places. You were a prosecutor; you were on the opposite side from these people. It isn't a question of whether they like you—you'll be a prize. Somebody can hurt you and brag that he bagged the prosecutor. I have seen cuts and rapes the guards never knew about."

He had my attention. "So what should I do?"

"When the correction officer comes back in, ask him about protective custody."

I did as the jailer suggested. I didn't think twice about it.

The meeting droned on for about another half hour, with at least half that time spent discussing Carolina football because the jailer had played for UNC-Chapel Hill in the early 60s.

After I went back downstairs, I was placed in a huge room by myself. I sat down on one of several wooden benches and leaned my head against the wall. I looked outside the locked glass doors and saw groups of black guys walking into another locked room, with the solid door held open by a white sheriff's deputy. He had clear latex gloves on his hands. Then the door slammed shut.

When the black inmates came out, they were happy and dressed in their civilian clothes. The officer kept changing his gloves, even though all he was doing was handling clothes.

Finally, after a three-hour wait, it was my turn. The sliding glass door opened, and I was asked to come outside. I walked through the same door as the others had. There was a shower to my left and an open window to the right where a black woman was standing.

"Mr. Blackburn, what size do you wear? You need to put this jumpsuit on, those socks, too. And, we've got some flip-flops."

I remembered a conversation Rick and I had one morning at breakfast back in the fall. "Jim, you've got to do what's best for you and let the chips fall where they may. You are the one who's going to wind up wearing one of those orange jumpsuits if you don't, not anybody else. I'm not going to jail. Marsha's not going to jail. You're the one going to jail, if you don't wake up."

Now I thought, "Well, Rick, I did what I thought was best for me, and I'm still going to wear an orange jumpsuit."

I looked down at the jumpsuit, sighed, and put it on, zipping up the front. Then, the guard handed me the longest, brightest orange socks I'd ever seen.

"You mean I've got to put these on also?"

"I'm afraid so, Mr. Blackburn, regulations."

I put them on. Finally came the black flip-flops. After my clothes were inventoried, I was ready to leave. If it is true that we are what we wear, then I had sunk to the bottom.

I didn't want to see anyone, nor anyone to see me. Maybe I could sneak out of the room and go quickly to my cell or wherever they were going to put me. Five seconds after the door opened, I heard someone yell, "Mr. Blackburn is to have a private cell on this floor tonight. I want his room checked every fifteen minutes. That's not for suicide watch but for security. Does everyone understand?"

Walking around the corner to my cell, I was stopped by a young female officer who told me that I had a visitor. Rick Gammon had returned to see how I was doing.

I was escorted to a booth with a stool behind it and an air phone on the wall. A glass partition separated us. He took one look at me and started laughing.

"Blackburn, if people could see you now, dressed like that."

"You son of a bitch. I thought I looked rather nice. What's the matter, you don't like orange?"

Rick turned serious. "How are you doing?"

"I'm okay. I think I'm going to Troy in the morning." We talked for about thirty minutes. Years later, I cannot remember our conversation, I only remember that he came. And that is all that is important.

Apparently, I had a suite that first night. I did not have to spend the evening with anyone else, and that fact alone made my cell a suite. It had a sliding door with a large window, one narrow bed with the thinnest mattress I had ever seen, and a sink in the back with a metal toilet attached to it. A short wall separated the toilet from the bed—and the view of everyone who passed by.

I was given a bunk roll for the night and told I could make up my bed. Unfortunately I put my head at the wrong end and was too nervous to change it. So I looked out at windows into the hall where officers walked, bathed in light, the entire night.

I didn't sleep very well that night. It takes a long time to close your eyes the first time in prison. Fatigue ultimately forces you to sleep. You can forget turning over, pulling up the covers, and fluffing the pillow.

Several days before, Wade told me, "Whatever you do in prison, Jim, don't find God, that's what Republicans do." I learned that night that God is bipartisan. He listens to Democrats as well.

A Stay in the British Empire

I had heard all the stories about prison—taking showers with other inmates and the dangers that lurked therein. So when I was asked early the next morning if I wished to take a shower, I said no. The officer persisted.

"Are you sure? I can put you in there before anyone else gets up. You can have it by yourself, and I'll lock the door."

"You'll lock the door?"

"Sure will. You can take your time."

I scrambled out of the bed and told the officer, "I'll be right there."

Later I was given the morning newspaper, which belonged to the magistrate. I was told I could look at it if I didn't mess it up. I saw the pictures and story from the afternoon before when I'd walked into the jail and been handcuffed for the first time.

The news attention became my friend. As long as someone was interested in writing about me or taking my picture, I would not be forgotten. I would have company along the way. So many people in jail or prison are forgotten. No one knows or cares that they are there. These are the most severe punishments of imprisonment: To be ignored or forgotten. To not be needed by the outside world. To lose your friends and family.

On this first full day in prison, I had a lot of time to think. I had been told that time in prison is a wasted time of your life. I had decided that would not be true for me. I wanted to gain something positive from all that was happening to me. I wanted to think about where I was going and what I wanted to do with the rest of my life. I decided not to sink into self-pity. I decided that to survive this experience, I had to be unafraid and even, on some level, to embrace imprisonment for as long as I was there. It was the best decision I ever made.

But first I had to get to Troy. As I walked out of the jail that morning, the jailer who had spoken with me the night before came up to me. As he put handcuffs around my wrists and shackles around my waist and ankles, he told me, "Mr. Blackburn, I want to wish you a lot of luck. This is just a temporary down for you. You have a lot of friends out there."

"Thank you a lot. I know that."

A young sergeant in a crisply starched brown uniform was my driver that morning. The two of us walked to a van parked in an enclosed lot next door to the jail. It was time to leave Raleigh.

The sun was bright. The weather was clear. Cars were moving on the road. Once again, I realized the awful fact that the world had not stopped while I had been away.

On this day, I felt an intense separateness from the city. It was out there. I could look at it, but I could not participate. I was no longer a part of it. I couldn't walk the streets or drive a car. If I asked the sergeant to stop, he wouldn't. If I tried to get out, I couldn't.

The ride to Troy took ninety minutes.

Several miles outside of Raleigh, our van pulled over to stop. The officer got out of the van, walked around the front, and opened the door to my side. "Mr. Blackburn, I don't know whether you want some coffee or not, but you're certainly welcome to some of mine. My wife made it for me this morning."

I looked at him with much gratitude. "I sure do."

"How do you like it?"

"However you got it."

He opened a brown thermos and poured what looked to me

like holy water into a cup and handed it to me. Coffee had never tasted so good. For a few moments, the handcuffs were no longer weights on my wrists. I remember the officer's warmth and kindness to this day. Even when you are at your lowest, you'll meet people who are kind.

"Tell me about Troy. What do you know about it?"

"Not too much. I've never worked there. It's relatively new and clean. It's a big place."

"I was told that I should ask for protective custody when I get there because I once was a prosecutor. You got any thoughts on that?"

"Sure do. Sounds like good advice to me. You never know who's out to get you. He can be your best friend one minute and turn on you the next. You don't need that. Somebody like yourself."

"That's what I thought you'd say."

Just as I was getting used to the van and my driver and our conversation, we turned off the main highway onto a narrow state road.

"How much further?"

"Oh, it's about three miles."

The Southern Correctional Center seemed to rise right out of the earth. Down the hill below the road emerged a large gray building surrounded by wire fences with tall guardhouses containing men carrying rifles. We drove slowly to the entrance and had to wait while a busload of newly arrived individuals walked into the prison to be processed. They had no chains around their ankles.

I got out of the van by myself, very carefully and very slowly. I still had the chains around my ankles, which I wore into the front entrance to the prison. That was a regulation. Because this was a medium-security prison, our uniforms were brown, but at least it was a shirt and pants, not an orange jumpsuit.

I was given my new clothes. I was able to keep my shoes, without the laces. I endured my first strip search and was sent on my way. The ankle chains were removed, and I walked with an officer to the area set apart for protective custody.

You know the old saying, "Beauty is in the eye of the beholder"? Well, what was considered protective custody for me was considered severe punishment for others. Protective custody means you're locked up by yourself all day except for forty-five minutes, which you can use to take a walk and a shower by yourself. You do not speak to or meet any other inmates. As a means of punishment it's called solitary confinement, but for me it meant that I did not have to worry about being safe.

Still, the day of processing was difficult. Remember how it is to go to a new school or a new job or a new town and walk into the place by yourself? You don't know anyone, and you don't quite know how to act. Multiply that by some huge factor, and you have my first day at Troy.

I learned to be polite, keep my mouth shut, and do whatever I was told. The first day was a series of meetings. First, I went to the doctor's office. There were two large rooms. In one, secured by a large glass door, were a number of inmates waiting their turn. I didn't have to go there but went straight inside the other room.

A young friendly nurse came up to me, stopped, and said, "I know you. You know who you look like? You look just like Jim Bakker."

"Who?"

"You know, Jim Bakker, the television evangelist who went to prison. You smile just like he does."

"Dear God. I don't need this. You've got to be crazy."

"Naw, I'm dead serious. You're a dead ringer for him if I ever saw one. Smile for me."

I smiled.

"See, I told you so. Jim Bakker."

I rolled my eyes. "So what do you want to do with me?"

She smiled. "Come with me, honey. Unbutton and roll up that sleeve. Let's take that blood pressure."

She wrapped the gauge around my arm and started pumping. "Um. Um. Um. Little high. You must be under a little pressure, darling."

I thought I was in love. I had found a friend. But my time was up. A man in a blue uniform came in and told us, "We're going to have to finish this later. He's got to go upstairs. See the psychologist."

With a new set of handcuffs on, my escort and I left for the next floor. We got off the elevator and walked toward a desk sitting in the middle of an open space. To my left was a large room with tables with lots of men standing around. To my right was a large open area with lots of doors like those on a ship. Before you could enter either room, iron bars had to slide open.

Seated at the desk was another man in a blue uniform. This one was called Sergeant. He had a graying beard and a distinctly unfriendly look. He was busy looking down at the top of the desk as he was writing on a tablet of paper.

"Who's this?" he said without looking up.

"Blackburn. He's in protective custody."

"Put him in C 1."

"He goes in cellblock C? Are you sure?"

The Sergeant looked up. "C 1."

"He's got to see the psychologist first."

"Okay. Are you going to stay with him?"

"Yes sir."

We turned and walked back toward a door that led to a small suite of offices. Inside, we walked to the end of the hall and opened the door to the right.

The psychologist was a fresh-faced little guy trying to act cheerful. I was not in the mood for happy talk that day. But I had nowhere I had to be other than with him, so I answered his questions about my medication, medical diagnosis, and what I'd experienced in the previous year.

After about an hour, we were done. I was on the way to my new home for the next several days. An officer told me they'd received a call about two visitors who wanted to see me the next day. For the first time that day, I smiled. Someone knew where I was and wanted to see me. That was all it took to give me hope.

As we walked back to the desk where I had first seen the sergeant, another officer came up to me and said, "Go through the door and up the stairs. Your cell is the first one on the left. We'll open the door, and you just walk through."

The door slid to one side, and I walked through the bars into cellblock C—except that it wasn't called that. Above the bars was a green and white sign that said England. I was in England. The Falklands were just next door. Imagine, a walking trip through the British Empire, here in the middle of North Carolina. The population consisted of a few people like me who were in protective custody and the rowdies—those who couldn't behave themselves and were troublemakers, banished to isolation. You wouldn't want to send postcards from here.

I walked across the open area to the metal stairs, climbed to the top, and turned left. About ten feet ahead, I turned back to the right and into my new home. As soon as I walked in, I heard a loud noise and turned around just in time to see my door sliding shut. I stared at the door. It was closed and locked all the way.

That door's closing and my being locked inside made me feel incredibly lonely. Separation and loneliness are what I think of when I remember those first days. I was around people, helpful people, but I was not among friends and family. That, to me, was the prison, that was the punishment.

I put my belongings on the floor and sat down on what passed for the mattress on a bed frame built into the wall. I looked around. As far as I could tell, it was clean. It was small. I had always read in books that inmates know the exact dimensions of their cell, so I tried to walk mine off. I wanted to conform. From the door to the wall with the window slits was about nine feet. From side to side was less, how much so depending on whether the sink and toilet or the small table attached to the wall was in the way. There were two slits that served as windows. They were each four inches wide and four feet high. On the wall near the sink was a light that stayed on all the time.

As I sat down on the bed again, I pulled out one of the bags that had been given to me containing the toiletries of prison. Inside I found a comb, safety razor, shaving soap, toothbrush, toothpaste, deodorant, shampoo, and nail clippers. I put the bag to the side.

That night, I again slept with my head facing the door. I guess I wanted to see who was going to come through the door.

I want to tell you about talking with God. I didn't get down on my knees and pray that night. I stayed in the bed with the blanket pulled up and stared at the locked door. I don't recall closing my eyes the entire night. But I do remember having a very long conversation with God. I asked for help in getting through all this with some degree of integrity and grace. In return, I simply promised to do the best I could, whatever that was. I did not believe that night that this prison term was the end for me. Rather, I believed, with all my heart, that if I could just survive this night, the rest of my prison sentence would be a new beginning.

I hadn't been so happy to see daylight since my last Boy Scout camping trip. I looked around and said to the room in general, "Thanks, God."

That morning, I had visitors, two friends from Raleigh, Sheila and Charlie, who had stuck with me through every critical turn of the entire previous year. They sat in one room and I in the other, separated from them by a large window. They brought news from home, letters from my children, and the sad news that our close friend Pete Carruthers did not have long to live. It was a sobering conversation.

Shortly after they left, I was taken back to the medical station. I saw my friendly nurse again, had my weight and blood pressure taken, and narrowly averted a complete medical examination because I was still under fifty years of age.

I spent the rest of the week in my cell. I ate my meals there, which were served through an opening in the door. I took my medicine on time as the nurses came around promptly at 4:00 A.M. Eagerly I awaited yesterday's newspaper, which a nurse gave me every day. I asked for anything else they had to read, too.

Another nurse gave me a small Bible. I read the stories that I remembered from the Old Testament, the beginnings of the earth, the flood, the time of Moses. I read about Paul and the establishment of the first Christian churches. I read about Eastertime and recalled the note from my law partner about each of us going through our own private Gethsemane.

I lay on my bed and thought a great deal. I went over the last two years in minute detail. I tried to reason everything out, so I could reach my own inner peace with where I was. And I was able to do that. When I walked the prison floors during my forty-five-minute stretch each day, I talked to myself and planned for the future.

Each day, I got stronger. Surviving those first hours and that first full day in prison made me feel better about myself. While I was there, I never turned on myself. Incredibly those days in protective custody were necessary to give me stability and perspective on what the next several months would require of me.

On Friday night, I received a call from Dr. Jean Spaulding. The officers allowed me to talk to her in their office and removed my handcuffs. On Saturday, the desk sergeant, who had been so businesslike and unfriendly when I arrived, had the door to my cell opened. He spent the better part of an hour standing in the doorway asking me questions about the MacDonald case.

I learned to listen for the rattling of pots and pans from down below in the open space. As soon as I heard them, I knew they were preparing a meal, and mealtime was a welcome break in the daily routine.

By the following Wednesday morning, I had been there eight long days. Boredom, the stuff of prison, had settled in. It was time for my transfer to Wake Correctional Center in Raleigh. I had just about given up hope it would happen this day. The sun was beginning to set, and soon the outside lights would be turned on, increasing the sense of isolation that I felt in prison. The lights to me were a form of control, a symbol that someone else was in charge. All day long I'd waited for the knock on my door to let me know that I was being transferred. Every so often, I looked out the slits in my cell door and watched for someone coming to let me out. Instead I heard the clanging noise of the kitchen crew setting up the line downstairs for our supper. That meant another night in isolation.

During the day, I'd noticed all the markings and drawings on the cinderblock wall and ceiling in my cell. They were all shapes and sizes. To me they represented people, wild things, and scenes from the farthest parts of my imagination. I had taken ink blot and other psychological tests during the past year., but I had never been this smart, to see so much in so little. I wanted to tell my doctor how bright I had become. Every time I looked at the wall, I saw something new. I was proving everyone wrong. Protective custody—in essence, solitary confinement—was not having a negative effect on me. It was making me brighter and more creative. It was also taking me into another world where my imagination was running wild and my focus was moving outward.

Suddenly, the tray in my door opened, and a woman's voice called out, "Mr. Blackburn, you need to be ready in ten minutes with your bags packed to go to Raleigh. You're going to be allowed to eat supper first, but hurry."

I put all my personal items in one bag. There weren't many. I had a Bible, a few letters from home, and the toiletry bag that the prison had given me. The larger bag I packed held the clothes and bedsheets that I was returning to the state before I left the building. As I stripped the sheets off the mattress, the cold, impersonal feeling of the jail returned. Seeing my cell for the last time, I felt a chill going through me as though I could not believe I'd actually lived here for over a week.

As I walked to the elevator, I tried to think of the appropriate words to say to the officers who were on duty. I imagined them telling me goodbye and wishing me luck or at least waving. No one said a word or even acknowledged I was leaving. The only person who spoke to me was an overweight older man in brown clothes with a long, gray beard.

"Hello, Mr. Blackburn, it's nice to see you. Good luck to you."

"Thanks." I wondered who he was and where I had seen him before. I never found out.

I rode the elevator down to the first floor with the unit manager. He was a short, bald man whom I had rarely seen during my eight days at Troy. He was pleasant enough but left no doubt as to why I was leaving his prison early.

"You sure do have a lot of friends."

"What do you mean?"

"Someone was always calling about you. They wanted to make sure you were taken care of. No doubt that *speeded up things* for you. Getting out of here in eight days is pretty fast. Usually takes about three weeks."

I'd hoped to see the nurses in the medical office one last time, but we didn't go by there. We reached the check-in office where I'd entered the previous week. A prison bus had just arrived with at least twenty-five new inmates.

"Where's the sergeant?" the unit manager asked.

"He'll be here in a minute. Why?"

"He's got to take Blackburn to Raleigh tonight. He's not going on the bus. He's to be in a car."

"Okay. Blackburn, sit over there. We'll be with you in a few minutes."

I watched the men getting off the bus. They weren't talking, joking, or smiling. They stood in a single line, waiting to take off their clothes, be searched, and receive brown clothes for their stay. Watching this process was not much less demeaning than going through it myself. Each person tried so hard to be silent and strong. I didn't speak to them, but I knew what was in their minds. They were afraid. They were humiliated. They were alone. They were in prison.

"Hey, Blackburn, over here."

"Yes, sir?"

"Give me your clothes. I've got to check you out."

"Again? Why, on the way out?"

"It's the way we do it. Come on, let's go."

And so, as this short, young man with dark, neatly combed hair stood by in his severely pressed blue shirt and pants, I once again took off each piece of clothing, only this time I was accompanied by a busload of new inmates. The officer looked at each article and threw it on a table nearby.

"Okay, put your clothes back on. You can go."

I went back into the office and sat down again and waited to be told what to do. I spoke to no one. I watched the blonde secretary trying to type and remain nonchalant as naked men walked by the door on their way to getting their new brown uniforms. Her typewriter was an old Royal that had to be thirty years old. It matched perfectly the decor in the room—state government down to the last key. The lowest section of government, an outpost prison in a small town in the middle of the state. All of us, the keepers and the kept, in a place no one wanted to be.

The sergeant finally walked in. "Hey, Blackburn, come over here. I've got to put these handcuffs on you."

I got up and walked a few feet to a desk where he was standing and held out my hands. He put the handcuffs on.

"Stand there a minute. I've got to put this chain around your waist and shackles on your ankles. Don't move."

I did as I was told. Then I sat down and waited to leave.

My transportation back to Raleigh was a four-door, blue Ford sedan, complete with a wire mesh separating the front and back seats. I had seen these cars a thousand times on the road, often carrying someone to jail. Now, it was my turn. With leg irons on my ankles, it was impossible to step normally into the back seat. I sat down on the seat and swung my legs inside. The sergeant leaned across me and fastened the seat belt. Then he checked out his car.

He opened the trunk, the engine hood, and looked under the car as well. He never said what he was looking for or whether this unnamed object was intended for him or me. Finally, we pulled away and slowly circled the prison as we took the same winding road out on which I'd entered the week before. I turned to look out my right window and watched the silent stone building recede in the distance. I saw no one outside and thought that odd until I remembered it was a prison, after all, and everyone was inside.

I looked at the trees, the grass, the billboards, even the road. I was quietly satisfied that I had survived my time in Troy, but I was apprehensive about what was ahead. My unit counselor had warned me all week about minimum-security camps.

"Mr. Blackburn, you should think about joining the regular population here just to get used to it. It's not going to be the same at Wake. There's going to be a lot of men in the same dorm, sleeping close together. You're going to eat together. You're not going to be ready for that unless you try it here first. But it's your decision."

I stayed where I was, in protective custody. I would face general population when I had to, and when I was ready, and not before. The silence of the week and the time alone had made me stronger, not weaker. Now, I would find out just how strong.

First Night in Raleigh Prison

We reached Raleigh and saw the traffic entering the city, and I looked at all those cars and wondered how the people inside them had lived their lives over the last days. How eventful had their time been? Had they had even noticed its passing? I watched the approaching city skyline, which mostly consisted of two new and competing office buildings reaching thirty stories into the air. Even with lights shining on them, the buildings looked cold and distant and empty.

As we turned onto the beltline surrounding Raleigh, I felt a growing sense of unease. I put my head back on the top of the seat and closed my eyes. I thought to myself, "It's going to be okay. You can't let anyone know you're scared. You're better than everybody thinks you are."

I opened my eyes and looked left. Across the road was an open area, bathed in lights, with red brick buildings and a large fence surrounding them. On the rolling grass in front was a lighted sign that read, "Wake Correctional Center." We turned into the driveway.

We drove up to a large fence. Behind it was a small brick gate center. Two officers came out.

My driver, a sergeant, spoke first. "I've got a prisoner from Troy to deliver to you."

"Who is he? What's his name?"

"Name's Blackburn, James Blackburn."

"We've been waiting for him most of the afternoon. We heard he was coming today."

I undid my seat belt and waited for my door to be opened. I almost fell down getting out, I was that happy to be out of that car. I felt as if I was returning from another planet. The officers stared at me as I walked clumsily through the gate into the prison.

"You can take those chains off him. He won't need those here."

This time the sergeant responded quickly. "Yes, let me undo those." First he took off the ankle chains and then the handcuffs and chain around my waist. I knew that the sergeant was only following regulations and correct prison procedure in locking me up so tightly, as was the guard who took me to Troy, but I wanted badly to tell him how stupid I thought it was. Just who in the hell was made safer by my being chained down as if I had killed someone? But I was quiet, polite, and said nothing but "Thank you, sir. Good luck to you."

I walked across a large paved area, through another opened gate, up a sidewalk, and into a building marked "Control Center."

"What's your name?"

"Blackburn, James Blackburn."

"Spell it."

"B L A C K B U R N."

"He's the guy everybody's been talking about coming. Hey, Blackburn, you're a lawyer, aren't you?"

"Used to be."

"Did they take your license?"

"I turned it in first, before they could take it."

"Listen, I'll bet you get it back."

"Thanks."

"We've got to get you some clothes, get you out of those brown things. Put you into some greens. Let's go to the laundry."

The laundry didn't take long. I took off my brown clothes and put on some green ones. I was given long white socks, long underwear, and a large brown coat with a large collar. I turned down a hat with earmuffs.

"Don't you want the hat?"

"I hate hats."

"But you're going to get very cold."

"I still hate hats."

Carrying my clothes and bed linens, I followed a sergeant out of the laundry, down a sidewalk bordered by gravel on one side and a bank of telephones on the other, toward some steps that led to K and L Dorm, which was where I was to stay.

The dorm had one center front door. The L side, which consisted of sixteen bunk beds, was on the right side. K side, a twin, was on the left. We turned first toward L side. The place was full. Everywhere I looked, I saw men dressed in green standing around rows and rows of iron bunk beds. The walls were dirty beige cinderblock. Bright fluorescent bulbs lit up the room.

As the sergeant and I walked inside, the room's noise level fell dramatically. Groups of three or four people, who just a moment before had been busily talking to each other, suddenly just stopped. Each man looked directly at me. I didn't know these people. I had no idea specifically why they were here, except, of course, they'd been convicted of a crime. When I had last spoken to this many convicted felons, I was a prosecutor in federal court, speaking against them at their sentencing hearing. I had often argued for active prison time, and usually they got it.

That first time I walked through L side, it felt like I moved in slow motion, as though it wasn't real. For over a year, I'd been tossed about, hitting one obstacle and then another, hoping each one was the last. But it was here, on the south side of Raleigh, less than a ten-minute ride from the city's downtown where I'd once worked and been welcome that the true struggle for Jim Blackburn began.

A few days ago, when my friend Charlie Hinton visited me in Troy, he told me that prison would either make me or break me, embitter me or raise me up. Twelve months before, Sid Eagles, another friend and now the chief judge of the state's Court of Appeals, had told me that "before a metal became gold, a lot of forging had to take place." In those few seconds after I entered the dorm and before I spoke to anyone, I knew that everything my family and I had been through in 1993 was to prepare us for this.

The early comments to me were open and friendly. One recognized me from television. Another asked if I weren't a famous prosecutor, then immediately asked if I thought Jeffrey MacDonald was really guilty. But not everyone rushed up. Many hung back and watched, their eyes signaling neither acceptance nor rejection, but cynical curiosity.

At the end of the L side tour, we reached the dorm's headquarters, which consisted of two large bathrooms, two dayrooms, and a large wooden desk at which an old man with large arms and neatly combed white hair was sitting. He wore a blue shirt and his gray pants had stripes on the sides. Just beneath his large black belt was a black can of mace, but no gun. Conversation was lively here, as he chatted with other inmates. He asked me to come speak with him in a few minutes.

The first person I met on K side was a gangly black man wearing jeans, a sweatshirt, and a tattered baseball cap.

I stuck out my hand to him. "Hi, my name's Jim Blackburn."

He told me his name. It sounded unintelligible, and I asked him to repeat it.

"Tell you what, you can call me Leroy."

"Fair enough, Leroy. I never would have remembered the other name you told me anyway."

He laughed, and I thought I had passed my first test.

"Blackburn, that's you over there."

"Where?"

"There, number 23, top bunk. That's all we have in here tonight. Tomorrow, we're putting you on a bottom one, probably on L side."

I put my bags and clothes down and threw the sheets and blanket on the top bunk. The sergeant shook my hand and left the building.

"Your locker's over there."

"Where?"

"That one over there, on the other side, one closest to the other bed."

I opened the locker, which was a tall open space with one shelf at the top, and a round bar just underneath. I had no hangers, so I started neatly placing my clothes inside. Before I was through, I'd changed to tossing everything in one pile.

"You want some help on the bed?"

I looked over at a young-looking white man with dark brown hair, dressed in green, and still wearing tan boots from working that day. He stood there, watching me closely.

"Sure, I could use some help."

"Let me show you how to do this. I'm only going to tell you once. You got to fold the ends like this. Make it look neat. Then, everyone will leave you alone."

After finishing the bed, he offered me some coffee. We sat down on the lower bunks to talk.

"Name's Ricky Carver. I'm from Durham."

"My name's Jim Blackburn."

"Where did they process you?"

"Troy."

"Yeah, that's where I went, too. Took me about three weeks. How long did you stay there?"

"Little over a week."

"What did you think of it?"

"It was clean, but I was ready to leave."

"You're sort of the new kid on the block. Let me give you some advice. Don't trust anybody here. They're all out for themselves. They want to get some edge that will help them go home. That's what it's all about. Except me, of course."

I laughed. "Sure," I said.

I walked with him to the dayroom where the hot water for coffee was kept. The guard motioned for me to come see him.

"Jim, my name is Harold Brown. I'm the dorm officer almost every day from 2:00 P.M. until 10:00 P.M. Now, I don't know you at all. All I know about you is what I've read in the paper and nothing else. Now, I've watched you since you came in tonight, and you seem like a nice enough fellow, but I want you to know that I don't play any favorites here. I treat everybody the way I would want to be treated.

"If you play fair with me, we won't have any problems at all. But, if you cause trouble, then I can cause trouble, too. Now, again, I don't expect we'll have any trouble, but I just thought it fair to let you know how I felt and where I'm coming from. I would tell anybody who came in here the same thing."

"Listen, Mr. Brown, I understand," I told him. "You're not going to have any problem with me. I can guarantee that. I appreciate your saying that to me. I didn't come here to change anything or do anything, other than what I'm supposed to do. I've got enough problems without having anything more to worry about."

"Well, please understand, I'm not being judgmental about what you did or allegedly did or anything like that. I just wanted you to know how I ran this dorm."

Ricky jumped in. "Mr. Brown, you're not harassing my new man here, are you?"

"No, Ricky, I'm not. I'm just trying to show him the ropes a little, if you don't mind."

"That's okay, Mr. Brown. I just wanted to make sure you're not upsetting him or anything. You know, he's one of us. It's been a long time since I had one of us on my side of the dorm. I mean, except for Joe Spence, I'm it. Nice to have a little white blood in here."

"You mean you don't like sleeping with all those blacks, those educated and well-mannered blacks in here?"

"Mr. Brown, I'm just glad to see my buddy Jim's here."

"I understand. You two go drink your coffee. Nice to meet you, Jim."

"Thanks, Mr. Brown."

"Brown's a good man. Runs the best dorm in the place. But he's totally in charge. He won't take any shit off nobody. If you're good to him, he's good to you."

"How long has he been here?"

"He's been in the system over twenty-five years. Used to be at Central. He was a tough customer over there. I've heard stories that would curl you."

"Ricky, I need to make a telephone call. How do I do that?"

"See Mr. Brown. He can give you a pass after hours. It's good for fifteen minutes."

I got my pass and walked outside into the darkness to the telephones below. Since I'd walked into Wade Smith's office eight days before, this was the first time I'd been outside alone. Walking. Outside. Alone. Before, in what felt like a different lifetime, I'd done it every day and taken it for granted. Now, on this cold Wednesday night in January, wearing a green shirt and slacks, on a fifteen-minute pass, inside prison fences, I walked alone. I felt wonderful.

No drug that I'd taken in the last year had made me feel this good. Before I reached the telephones, I stopped, bent down, and touched the grass. I let the blades of grass run through my hands and thought about how much I had missed that.

I called my house. A soft, quiet, female voice answered.

"Hey, kid."

"Daddy, is that you!"

"Sure is. How are you?"

"I'm okay. Where are you?"

"I'm in Raleigh. I just got here."

"You're in Raleigh? Are you sure?"

"I think so. It looked like Raleigh when we came in."

"Daddy, I love you, Daddy."

"I love you too."

Left to right: Marsha and Stacy were at home together while I was in prison and Jeff was in college

"Are you really in Raleigh? When can we see you?"

"I'm really in Raleigh. At Wake Correctional. Maybe I can see you this weekend. Listen, how's school?"

"It's doing okay. I sure have missed you, Daddy."

"Well, let me tell you, I have missed you, too. I sure have. Stacy, is Mom there?"

"No, she's at a school meeting tonight."

"Well, tell her I'm back, and I'm okay, and that I'll call tomorrow."

"Okay. Good night, Daddy. I love you."

"I love you too, kid. Talk to you tomorrow."

I hung up the receiver, turned, and walked out of the telephone booth into the cold night air. The sky was clear and the stars were out. I walked slowly back to K and L Dorm. I was on a high from a brief conversation with my fourteen-year- old daughter. Stacy has high standards. If she still liked me, even in prison, maybe all was not lost.

Walking back into the dorm, I heard Mr. Brown call out, "Count time in K side dayroom. Let's go. Everybody in there. Now!"

Wake had no guard towers, so the guards kept track of every-one by counting them four times a day. We all walked into the K side dayroom and then back out again, as he counted us off one at a time. About ten minutes after the count began, we heard the sergeant's voice over the loudspeaker in the dorm.

"The count is clear. The count is clear." And for a few more minutes, the dorm returned to normal.

At 10:00 P.M., the new dorm officer on duty for the remain-der of the night walked to the front door and flicked the switches that shut off the lights. All conversations around beds had to stop, and inmates had two choices: go to bed or go to the day-room, where we could watch television, play cards, or read. I went to bed.

Before I went to prison, friends asked me if I was worried about my safety. Even the local newspaper speculated about that. As a prosecutor, I'd sent people to jail. How would I be treated when I got there? Would I be safe at night? I had no private room or cell or even a small area with only a few people around me. This was wide open. But I was so tired I fell asleep within min-utes.

It wasn't fifteen minutes before I felt someone pushing on my leg. I opened my eyes slowly and looked up. Five black faces stared at me. I sat up.

"Mr. Blackburn," one of them whispered. "We know it's late and this is your first night and all, but you know, we would sure like it if you would find the time sometime to tell us about that

Jeffrey MacDonald trial. That must have really been something. We're just glad you're here. I mean, you must have been the man. Do you think you'd mind talking to us?"

I looked at them and nodded. "I'll tell you what. We can do that tomorrow. I don't mind at all."

"Thanks, Mr. Blackburn, we'd appreciate that. It isn't too often we have someone in here like you. That would be real nice."

I lay back down and, for the second time, went to sleep.

Mr. Matlock

On my first morning there, a Thursday, the lights came on at 5:00 A.M. I thought, "This is when we get up? Are you serious? Good God."

I looked outside and it was dark. I was on the top bunk, so I looked around to see what was happening. The answer was: not much.

All of a sudden, I heard yelling.

"I slept like a motherfucker last night. What the hell's the weather like? Damn, I bet it's as cold as a motherfucker out there. Shit."

"What are you talking about, Leroy?"

"None of your fucking business, preacher."

"Heh, heh, heh, God is good, Leroy. Yes, sir, God is good. And he's going to get you. Talking like that. You better start reading that Bible, I'm telling you."

"Preacher, why don't you stop that crap, at least at this time of the morning. Damn, I hate this motherfucking weather."

I sat up in my bed. Most people were still under their covers, paying little or no attention to Leroy and the preacher. Those two were like a bad radio station that you learned to tune out. But I got down from my bed, threw my towel over my shoulder, and walked between them on my way to the showers.

Four showers were at the back end of the bathroom. The water was hot, and I was alone. Almost everyone else was still in bed. Walking out of the bathroom, I noticed a black man on his knees just off to my right. He wore a round hat, knelt on what looked like an old Oriental rug, and swayed up and down. I soon learned he was a Muslim in the midst of his morning prayers. He slept two bunks down and across the aisle from me.

Ricky liked to push it, staying as late as he could in bed. He worked in area maintenance, which meant heavy manual labor at times, so a morning shower was not uppermost in his mind.

"You going to breakfast, Ricky?"

"Yeah, I don't know why. Maybe they're having cereal or something I can eat this morning. You haven't lived until you try breakfast here. Unbelievable. Can't eat the stuff most mornings."

I felt pretty good. I'd spent a night in my third prison, which would be my new home for a few months. I had slept in a prison dorm, taken a shower, shaved with a safety razor. I'd made a few friends, not made anyone mad, and survived. I was ready for breakfast, and I didn't have to be served through a hole in the door. Man, I was tough. I was cool. Hell, prison wasn't so bad. And then I walked outside.

A little after 5:30 on a cold, gray Thursday morning, I saw prison for the first time.

Just beyond the fenced-in grounds was Rock Quarry Road, already beginning to breathe into life this morning with new traffic breezing by. I could see the stoplights in the distance, changing colors, telling drivers when they were free to go and when they should stop. A mile to the right was the beltline encircling the city, on which I had traveled many times. I looked at the faces of the men around me, walking in small groups to the dining hall, and saw resignation, if not defeat. Sadness, if not bitterness. During my entire time in prison, I never once saw a happy person or a happy moment, with the sole exception of the moment someone was leaving.

We stood in line around the dining room walls, waiting to reach the food service area. I saw a bearded man with long hair and dark glasses look my way in recognition. I started to wave until I heard him speak.

"Ricky, you better look out and be careful. That's the Mac-Donald man, he's out to get people like us."

Others looked up from their meals and said, not too softly, "That's the prosecutor, that one over there," while pointing directly at me.

I turned to Ricky. "Who the hell is that?"

"Don't worry about him none, he's crazy. Nobody pays any attention to him."

"Why would he make a big deal about me?"

"You don't know, do you?"

"No."

"You were a famous prosecutor. You were on the side of law enforcement. You helped put people in prison. But hell, that was your job, and I don't have any problem with that. Matter of fact, I respect you for doing your job. But some of these guys don't think that way. They just think everybody with law enforcement is bad, and they don't trust anybody like that."

"Great. Law enforcement helped send me here, and they don't like it because they think *I'm* law enforcement."

We reached the serving line.

"Hey, Blackburn, how you doing this morning?"

I looked up and saw an officer standing by the trays and grinning.

"I'm okay. How you doing?"

"Not bad, not bad."

I got two eggs, fried hard, and turkey sausage, grits, two pieces of bread lightly browned to resemble toast, and jelly. Coffee was on the outside.

I sat at a table with Ricky and two others.

"Well, how does it feel to be the big man on campus this morning?"

"Is that what I am?"

"Afraid so. You're the only celebrity we got."

"Terrific."

"Hey, Jim, what's it like, you know, being on this side? Never thought you'd be here, did you?"

"No, I never did. It's just different. Nobody I know would believe this."

"What?"

"You know, wearing the clothes, standing in line, no privacy," I answered.

"All of them blacks. Hey, Jim, did you ever see so many in one place? I mean, it's something."

"Look at those in the line," one of the inmates said. "I bet not a one is over twenty-one years old. They think this place is a party. They come in here for a few months, then the Parole Commission lets them out; they do drugs, steal something, or hurt somebody, and, boom, they're back in. Me, I'm white. You think somebody's going to let me out early? Not hardly. Wrong skin color."

I just sat there and listened.

"Jim, are you eligible for work release?"

"Yeah, the court recommended it. I may be close to having it set up, I don't know. I've got to work on that today. How do you do that?"

"Oh, they call you. You don't call them. Your programmer is supposed to get with you within the first week and start getting your paperwork ready for work release, if you're eligible. You probably are."

"That's right, they're not going to mess much with you. They don't want you around here."

"Why do you say that?"

"You're too high-profile for them. They're going to be afraid of you."

"Why?"

"Jim, you know too many people. When you're outside, you might talk about them. They don't want that."

"Look, all I care about is doing my thing and getting out of here. I'm not interested in saving the world."

We finished breakfast, and I walked back to the dorm. I climbed on my bunk and closed my eyes. It wasn't yet 6:30 in the morning. Over the next hour and a half, I watched more than half of my roommates leave for work, either on work release or work for the prison system, such as building maintenance or cleaning the grounds. It was about 8:00 A.M. and the dorm was quiet. A new dorm officer came on duty just then.

"Hey, Blackburn, you don't have a job yet, do you?"

"No, not yet. I hope to soon."

"Well, those that don't have a job outside work here in the dorm every day. How about getting one of those brooms and sweeping the K side of the dorm, under the beds and all."

I got a broom and a dustpan and did as I was told. It didn't take long, and I didn't spend much time thinking about what I was doing. I just did it, but after I was through, I walked outside thinking, I'm not going to get anywhere sweeping floors. I needed to get out of view of anyone who could give me another chore and keep me too busy to figure out how to get my work release. After knocking on doors and filling out a paper request, I got an audience early that afternoon with my programmer, a recent graduate of East Carolina University who had majored in criminal justice. Dena was from the small eastern North Carolina town of Trenton, long known as the home of a former chief federal district court judge who had presided over some of my cases. She listened to my request for work release as soon as possible.

My case moved swiftly. A few telephone calls to the law firm of Morgan and Reeves and to Robert Morgan, and my work release was set for the next day. Word moved fast, and by nightfall, I had a new reason for celebrity: fastest work release given. My fellow inmates were less than unanimous in their feelings of happiness for me, but at this point, I didn't care. Self-preservation was taking priority over making everyone like me.

My assignment to work for Robert Morgan brought me full circle. When I was twenty-five years old and fresh out of law school, he had given me my first job as a lawyer in the attorney general's office. He used to brag that the first five people he hired had done well. One was now a supreme court justice, another a superior court trial judge, two were successful private attorneys, and then there was me. For a long time, I had been the most spectacularly successful. Now, in my mind and surely in others, I had also failed spectacularly. In thinking about myself, I often used the expression "damaged goods." It was not with a lot of confidence that I walked into work on Friday morning.

"Well, hello, Dr. Blackburn."

He always called me that. "Hello, Senator. How are you doing?"

"I'm all right. The question is, how in the world are you?"

"I'm okay."

Robert laughed. "You can't possibly be 'okay,' staying in prison. How have you been treated so far?"

"Actually, all right. Everybody's been fairly nice and understanding. Food's lousy, everybody wears the same-looking clothes, a lot of dumb rules. Except for the fact that it's a total disgrace, I'm doing well.

"Listen, Senator, I hope it doesn't cause you any problem, me being up here. I'm not exactly king of the world right now."

"I'll put it this way. If somebody doesn't like it, they can kiss my you-know-what. The time when you need your friends is when you're down, not when you're on top. If I can't be your friend now, I'm not much good to you. Everybody can be nice to you when you're riding high."

Somebody said, "Jim, somebody's here to see you," and I turned around.

"Hello, Wade Smith."

"Aren't you Jim Blackburn?"

"I used to be."

"Well, Jim, it's good to see you," he said as he gave me one of his oversized bear hugs. "I even like your new haircut," referring to the closer-than-usual cut that a prison barber had given me the day before.

"Come on in and sit down," I said, showing him into my office that stood between Robert's office and his daughter Margaret's. This was a family firm. Robert's son-in-law was one door further down, and I was actually using his daughter Mary's office while she was away on maternity leave.

I told Wade, "It's been a long eight or nine days. People have been very nice to me, almost unbelievably so. I've told myself this many times, but prison really is a mental thing. I mean you have to steel yourself to where you are, and what you are doing, and not let them have all or even very much of you. If you can do that—and you have to work at it—you can survive. You have to be strong. There's so much time to think that you've got to learn to like yourself or at least deal with yourself."

"What's the worst thing you've had to go through?"

"I don't know. I guess it's the separation from everyone you know and the feeling, no, the knowledge, that you're not in control. You have to do what someone else says. That's tough."

"What do you think is the best thing?'

"Coming back to Raleigh. Days passing . . . no, I think the best thing I've learned is that I'm tougher than I thought I was, than anybody thought I was. You know, Wade, I don't like this. I don't like anything about this. But, I can do it. And, I'm going to do it. The right way. No asking for special anything. Then, someday, it will be over, and no one can say anything to me about how I did it."

"Jim, you're exactly right. I am so glad you think that way. You know, in the thirty years that I've practiced law, this may be the greatest experience I've ever had. Think about what we were facing. Absolute destruction. Of everything. Think about what you've been through."

"Wade, this is the easy part. Prison, compared to last year, is no problem. I know that's hard to understand."

"Not to me. I was there, I remember. You know, this is almost the perfect defense case."

"What do you mean?" I asked.

"Think about it. From the beginning, we realized something was terribly wrong with you or this would not have happened. We took care of you. We got you the best doctor we could find. That became more important than the case.

"And then, we held our head high. We walked right through the storm. We took their best shot. They didn't give us a thing, not one thing. And we took it. And I believe that's why you're doing so well now. Don't get me wrong. This strategy would never ever have worked with ninety-nine percent of the clients in the world. But it did with you. We agreed to do the right thing and to hell with it. Just to hell with it. Not many people could do that. Not many. I am really proud of you."

"Thanks, Wade. I guess, if you want to know the truth, I'm proud of me, too. I know last year wasn't easy for any of us, and I wasn't always the best client. And I wasn't always appreciative. But, you know that I am."

"Jim, I know that. Listen, the whole thing's a miracle, that we got to this point."

"You got that right."

Our conversation soon ended, and Wade left to return to his law practice down the street. I turned to my own tasks, gingerly touching buttons, so to speak, to see what worked in this prison world of work release. I still had miles to go. This morning was just the beginning, and it was still very cold outside.

Late that day, about 7:00 P.M., Margaret Morgan took me back to prison. She was thirty-three years old, a very good lawyer, and every inch her father's daughter. She was smart, impatient, and possessed his strong trait of loyalty. She was on my side.

I couldn't help but think as we left the law offices building of another day eighteen years before, on election night in 1976, when she watched the returns while sitting on the floor at our house, eating hamburgers from McDonald's, before seeing her father later that night, then the junior United States Senator from

North Carolina. This night, as I walked across the street to her car, I looked around to see if I recognized anyone. I was glad that I didn't and felt relieved when we'd left the downtown area.

As I got out of her car at the prison, I walked to the gate and hoped that the guard inside would quickly open the door so that I would not have to stand there long waiting to get in, with Margaret watching. I was lucky; there was no wait and Margaret left.

Once inside the first gate, the officer on duty came around and patted me down to make sure I was not bringing any contraband back into prison. This search was routine and was conducted every time I returned to prison.

I walked up the sidewalk, past the control center, and near the bank of telephones. Even though it was dark and cold, the ten telephones were in full use, as they would be throughout the night until the yard closed. Walking up the steps, I passed a well-built black man who looked at me, didn't smile, and said, "Matlock."

That was it, just the name of a popular television show about a lawyer named Matlock. It starred Andy Griffith as the title character and was filmed mostly in Wilmington, North Carolina.

I turned around. "You want something?"

He glared at me again and said, "Maybe. I'll let you know, Matlock."

"Okay," I said and turned back to the dorm.

I put my hands in my pockets and my head down to ward off the wind. Just as I climbed the last steps to the dorm's warmth, I looked up and saw another, older black man, this one lean and wiry, with a dark beard covering his face. He was waiting for me.

He was a head taller than me, and there was no smile on his face. He spoke first, "I understand you're a lawyer."

"I used to be."

"Listen, I've got a problem. I come up again before the Parole Commission real soon, and I've written this letter to them. It's about myself, and why I think I deserve to be paroled this time.

The only thing, is, I'm not sure I've said it very well. I can talk pretty good, but, you know, I can't write real well. You think you might be willing to look over it for me and tell me what you think?"

"Do you have the letter with you?"

"Yes, sir, I got it right here."

He pulled out two crumpled sheets of paper and stuck them in my hand. He looked at me with a seriousness and a pleading that I had not seen in a long time.

"Tell you what. If you'll give this to me, I'll take it and read it tonight. I can see you tomorrow, maybe at breakfast, and let you know what I think. How's that?"

The old man sighed. "That sure would be mighty nice of you, if you would do that for me. I can't spell or write too well, so please don't be too surprised at that."

I smiled back. "Don't worry, if you can think it, I can write it. We'll get this done. Now, it's cold. I think I'm going inside." We shook hands.

I stuck the papers in my pocket and walked inside K and L Dorm. Ricky was sitting on his bunk, polishing his tan boots. Smitty, otherwise known as Anthony Tyrone Smith from Wilmington, a thirty-five-year-old repeat offender for theft and breaking and entering, was my bunkmate below. He was stretched out on his bed, resting his eyes.

A friend of Ricky's from the L side of the dorm, Dwight Pruitt, was sitting on a chair between the two bunks. Dwight was about thirty years old, from Raleigh, and in prison on a probation violation. He was big, strong, lifted weights regularly, and stayed in trouble because he didn't know how to think lawfully. He had wavy brown hair, a mustache, and, when he wanted, an infectious smile.

Dwight was the first to greet me. "Hey dude, what's happening? How was working in the senator's office? Probably beats the shit out of staying here."

"It does. How you guys doing?"

"Oh, just lovely," Ricky said. "This is just where I like to spend my Friday nights."

Dwight looked at me and laughed. "You got a big weekend planned?"

"Me? Yeah, thought I might go to the movies tomorrow night. You know, when you work for a former senator, the Department of Correction gives you special time off, such as weekend passes to go wherever you want to."

Dwight stopped grinning. Ricky looked up, and even Smitty raised his head to one side. Dwight spoke first. "Are you serious?"

"Sure. I'm getting some more clothes brought in tonight . . ." I looked at their stricken faces. "Of course I'm not serious. You think I'm crazy? If I had that kind of influence, you think I'd be here tonight? Not on your life."

Just then, I saw Mr. Brown motioning to me from his desk.

"Excuse me, guys, I'm being summoned."

I walked the thirty feet to the front of the dorm where Mr. Brown spent the majority of his evenings. "Well, Jim, did you enjoy your first taste of freedom, limited though it was, in the big city today?"

"Yeah, I did. It felt different."

"In what way?"

"I don't know. It was good to get out, to see people, to use the telephone, go to a normal bathroom, ride in a car without handcuffs on me, walk on the sidewalk. Strange. I didn't know quite how to handle it at first."

"Yeah, I imagine all of this is right much of a shock to someone like yourself, being locked up and all."

"Sure as hell is. I never thought I'd be in prison. Not in a million years."

"Well, listen, I don't know what you had for supper, but Mrs. Brown did some cooking this afternoon and made some extra biscuits if you'd like some. Might taste good with your coffee later on."

"Gosh, thanks, Mr. Brown."

"Now, you don't have to take them unless you want to."

"I'll take them! Thanks."

"Well, I see Mr. Brown's looking after you, tonight," someone said when I returned to my bed.

I looked around and saw Ricky cleaning his boots, a sly grin on his face.

"He does that every now and then, if he likes you, if you become one of his boys."

"I'm ready to do that."

"Figured you would be. Anybody coming to see you tomorrow for visitation?"

"Yeah, I think the whole family's coming, Marsha, Jeff, and Stacy."

"Here, take this." He tossed me a T-shirt. "It's new, never been worn. You got to look good for your first visitation."

"Where did you get this? It has a pocket on the front and everything. I haven't seen any of these."

"Ike, over in L Dorm, looks after me, does my laundry every week for three dollars. You ought to speak to him, get him to do yours."

I looked at the new T-shirt he'd just given me. It was clean white and the right size. I folded it neatly, put it in my locker, and saved it for Saturday.

"Jim, we've got to get you looking the part tomorrow before your family comes."

"Hey, Dwight, what you got in mind?"

"Well, I've got these round dark glasses and a great scarf. It's red, white, and black, got a skull and crossbones. You can tie it around your head and go out and growl at them. Then, maybe they'll be scared to death and will somehow get you released."

I laughed. "Give me a few weeks, Dwight. Right now, I don't think so. But check with me again."

"Jim, I've got to tell you. You're all right. For a famous lawyer, you're not bad. You might make it on the inside after all."

"Dwight, that's what I live for."

Saturday, January 15, was the beginning of my first weekend back in Raleigh. A Raleigh newspaper, the *News and Observer*, had a story on the local page about my getting work release within two weeks of entering prison. At that time, Wake Correctional Center had between 300–400 inmates. By lunchtime, everyone there had either read or heard about the story. Many of them didn't know how to treat me. Some ignored me, others spoke or nodded and went on, and a few were friendly. But almost everyone felt that I was given special treatment.

"Twenty-four hours, I'd say that's a record," said an older white man, with thinning gray hair and a towel wrapped around his shoulders, as he walked to the shower Saturday morning.

"Who's that?" I asked Ricky.

"Name's Joe Spence. He's been here about three years, sleeps on our side near the wall. He's been down for almost twenty-eight years."

"Twenty-eight years! What in the world did he do?"

"Murder. Got a life sentence. Used to be on death row."

"Great. And he sleeps two bunks away?"

"Yeah, but he's harmless. Actually, a rather nice old man, but he keeps pretty much to himself."

"You see the story in the paper, Ricky?"

"Yeah, I read it. Didn't bother me none. Public's going to drive you crazy if you let them. I mean, you pleaded guilty, you're doing your time. They need to let you alone. But they won't do it. They want all the pounds of flesh they can get."

"I know . . . I know."

A Saturday Night Dance

It was like a high school dance. Every prisoner who was eligible to have a visitor on Saturday—which meant those whose last names started with an initial falling in the first half of the alphabet—showered, shaved, and put on the cleanest green outfit he could find in his locker. Hair was combed or brushed, even aftershave was used. Shoes were polished, belts were donned, and everybody sat down and waited, like girls at a high school gym dance in the 1950s.

On visitation day, your best friend became the voice on the loudspeaker who called out your name to come to the dining hall for this long-awaited date. If your call didn't come promptly at starting time, which was 12:30 P.M., that was okay because you didn't want to appear overeager. You wanted to be cool about this, as though you could take it or leave it.

But if the long hand reached one, 1:00 P.M. or later, and still no invitation to dance, a funk set in like you have never seen. Loneliness is a definition of prison, and visiting days in prison spent without family or friends were the hardest days of your sentence.

I sat on my top bunk in K and L Dorm, waiting. At about 12:45 P.M., I heard my name called. I walked into the dining hall and saw Marsha, Jeff, and Stacy over to my right. They had brought a hang-up bag of clothes for me to wear to work, and a guard

161

had to inspect the bag before they could sit down at a table with me.

"How are you doing?" Marsha asked.

"I'm all right, it's not so bad. I've been treated fairly well by everyone."

"Have you? All your friends are worried sick about you. Do you feel safe here?"

"Yeah. I don't think that's going to be a problem. One of the guards even brought me some food last night."

"One of the guards brought you food?" Stacy asked, looking incredulous.

"That's right, two biscuits. I had coffee with them."

"Dad, you're the only person I know who could go to prison and have a guard bring you food."

"Well, it was pretty good. I hope to keep it up. Who knows? How do you-all like my haircut?"

"It's a little short," Jeff said.

"A little short. You call this a *little* short? You're damn right it's short. Look at my eyebrows. He even cut my eyebrows. They do that in prison. Can you believe that?"

Stacy commented, "Dad, green is not your color."

I laughed. "It is now, kid, it is now."

Marsha spoke up. "Who are all these people?"

"Marsha, the ones in green live here. The others get to leave when the bell rings."

"I know, but so many of them look so young."

"They are young."

Just then, a woman who was visiting an inmate who lived in my dorm, walked over to our table. "I understand my son is in your dorm, Mr. Blackburn. I know you are a good man. I wish you would talk to him when you can and try to help him. He needs someone with maturity to help straighten him out. He's a good boy. He just let a woman mess him all up."

"I know your son. He sleeps close to where I do. When I can, I'll try to talk with him some, I promise."

Left to right: Jeff and Stacy, taken when he was a senior and she a sopho-more at Wake Forest University

She grabbed my hand and thanked me. "I do hope everything goes well for you from here on out."

"Thank you."

As she walked away, Marsha asked, "What's her son in for?"

"I think he got six years for stalking his ex-wife. They have two children. She left him, and he's having trouble handling it."

"Six years, I'd say so."

"Seems pretty nice, but he spends a lot of time just sleeping. He keeps to himself."

Marsha looked at me with concern. "Are you taking your medicine? Are you getting it on time?"

"Yeah. Who would have believed it? I get the medicine like clockwork every morning, Prozac, lithium, and the Provacol for cholesterol. I got it regularly at Troy, too. They would even stand there and watch me take it."

"Dad, is anybody giving you any trouble?"

"No, not really, Stacy. There's one guy who's sort of ugly, with a long beard. He hasn't been real pleasant. But everyone else has. They don't know what to make of me yet. Oh, see that guy over there. That's Ricky. Lives next door. Helped me make up my bed the first night. I think that's his mother and sister from Durham."

"What's he in for?" Jeff asked.

"I'm not real sure. Something about being a terror to the public. Actually, I think he was in a high-speed chase with the police and then had the misfortune to point a shotgun at one of them, or so they said. He got six years. He's really been screwed by the system. He's going to have to max out his sentence, which means, by the time he gets out, he will have done almost two full years. That's a long time."

There was an inevitable pause in the conversation. We'd made the obligatory small talk that broke the tension of the occasion. This was the first time either Marsha, Jeff, or Stacy had seen me in prison, much less dressed in prison clothes. I was meeting them in a huge dining hall with no privacy except that afforded by huddling around a small table and chairs.

They'd had to sign in, along with all the other visitors, and pass by guards as they did so. They were ill at ease, though they tried hard not to show it. Jeff and Stacy smiled and tried to be upbeat and kidding. Marsha tried also, but she cried once. They wanted very badly to give me support and let me know that they still loved me, still believed in me, and were still on my side.

I simply tried to make them feel at ease. I was so grateful for their visit. I knew how hard it was for them to hold their heads high and be with me. But it was no different for them than it was for any inmate and his family.

Dorm Life

After leaving the dining hall, I stopped by the canteen for a cup of coffee. Even though the weather was cold, a number of other inmates were huddled together outside, smoking cigarettes and listening to boom boxes. Coffee was a dime. The guy behind the counter liked to say it was as good as Shoney's.

As I was walking back to the dorm, I heard a familiar voice.

"Hey, Matlock."

I turned around and saw the same black man from two nights before. "Yeah? What can I do for you?"

"Hey, Matlock, you and me. We got to talk."

"Talk about what?"

"You know, things."

"No, I don't know, things. Why don't you tell me."

"Hey, man, this is hard for me. You're white, I'm black. You're somebody. I'm not nobody. I need your help. I'm from South Carolina, and I don't know anyone here. I want to get closer to home, if I can."

"Okay, but it's cold right now, and my coffee's getting that way. See me at supper. We'll talk after that."

His tight face finally eased a bit and his eyes looked a little less cold. "Okay, I'll find you after supper. And thanks."

"It's okay."

We spoke later, but unfortunately I was not able to help him. He was soon sent even farther away, in fact, to the Midwest, due to prison overcrowding.

I walked back into K and L Dorm, slowly went to my bunk, took off my coat, and climbed on top to lay down. I had just closed my eyes when I heard a soft voice calling my name. I opened my eyes and looked around, right into the sad face of my bunkmate, Smitty.

"Hey, uh, Jim. I know you're doing okay and all, and I was just wondering if you could spare me a little money. You know, make me a small loan."

"Sure, Smitty, what do you want?"

"Well, I think five dollars would stand me in real good stead."

"Okay, let me get it for you." I climbed down off the bed, opened my locker, and handed him a five dollar bill.

"Jim, ain't you got no lock?"

"No, I don't. You think I need to get one?"

Smitty started laughing. "Man, these boys will steal you blind if you don't lock it up. I mean, lock everything up. And another thing, I noticed you taking a shower this morning."

"Yeah?"

"Well, Jim, it's none of my business, but you were walking barefoot."

"So?"

"Jim, don't ever walk barefoot in this place. God knows what kind of disease you'll get."

"Are you serious?"

"Man, Jim, for somebody as smart as you are, you need to learn about prison. Lock all your stuff up, keep to yourself, and wear shoes."

I laughed. "Okay, Smitty. I promise I'll do what you suggest, and I'll buy a lock."

"Well, until you do, here's an extra lock. Now, the thing is, it doesn't work, but nobody knows that. It'll close and look like it's locked. This will probably keep people from trying you."

I took the lock, slipped it on my locker and it looked perfect. Only Smitty and I knew it was worthless.

"Another thing, Jim, you need a shelf for your locker. I noticed your stuff isn't too neat in there."

"Smitty, is there anything you haven't noticed?"

He grinned, "Well, Jim, these are pretty close quarters, you know. When I'm lying on my bed here, I can see about everything."

"Okay, so what do you suggest?"

"Let me find a shelf for you, and I'll put it in for you."

"And how are you going to do that?"

"Jim, you just sit back, relax, and watch. I can do some things that even you can't do."

"Smitty, I don't doubt that at all, not for a moment."

One of the guys called to me, "Hey, Blackburn, somebody at the door wants to see you."

I got down off my bunk and walked to the front door and opened it.

"Jim Blackburn?"

"Yeah."

"My name's Carl Poole. I'm Brantley's brother."

Brantley Poole was a Raleigh man, a former member of the Real Estate Licensing Board that I once represented when I worked for the attorney general's office in the early 1970s. Brantley was a successful real estate broker in his own right, and I often saw him at lunch at a favorite local eating place called The Profile.

The man in front of me was thin with gray hair. He wore dark glasses. Brantley was large with thinning white hair and never wore glasses. I stepped outside and took off the man's glasses.

"You're Brantley's brother, all right. You have the same eyes. What are you doing in prison?"

"Oh, I had some money problems a while back involving my ex-wife. I didn't handle it well and ended up here. I'm supposed to get out soon. But I talked to Brantley this morning, and he asked me if I had seen you. He told me to look after you and make sure you're all right. Says you're a good man. Brantley likes you."

"Yeah, Brantley and I used to be buddies, a long time ago."

"That's what he said, too. Listen, is there anything I can do for you?"

"I don't think so."

"There is one thing I can do. Wait here. Give me your coat. I'll be right back."

I took off my coat and went back inside. In about five minutes, Carl was back with another coat.

"Here, try this one. It's new and a little larger. Yes, sir, that fits you a lot better. You can keep that. I told you I could help you. See, I used to work in the prison system. I know more about it than most of the staff here. They're all the time asking me questions about how to do things. If you need something, holler, and I'll get it for you."

"Thanks, Carl. I appreciate that."

I walked back inside wearing my new coat.

"Where'd you get that new coat, Jim?"

"Carl Poole just went and got it. Didn't seem to be a problem."

Ricky continued. "You'd better watch him. He probably wants something. He's always talking about who he knows. He wants to know you. Probably thinks it will help him get out."

I laughed. "I don't think I can help anybody right now. I'm pretty much at the bottom."

"Yeah, but you know people on the outside who are important."

"I used to know people on the outside who are important. I doubt if they know me right now. You know, I don't think there's anything lower than somebody in prison. You don't have any rights. You do what people tell you to do. You eat and sleep on a schedule. You got the influence of an ant. You know, Ricky, on Monday I will have been in prison for two weeks."

Suddenly I heard another voice. "Two weeks. I've been in twenty-six years. I've sat on the commode in there longer than two weeks. That ain't nothing."

"Hello, Joe. You know Jim?"

"Oh, we haven't been properly introduced, but I've heard about him. Nice to see you. I'm Joe Spence."

"Hey, Joe. I guess you have been in here a long time. When did you start?"

"You mean, when did I first come to prison?"

"Yeah."

"In 1966. I was twenty-six years old. I came in, was on death row for four and a half years."

"You were what?"

"Death row, over at Central."

"Dear God. Would you be willing to tell me about that sometime?"

"Sure, if I'm not doing anything, just ask me, and we can talk. I'm not going anywhere."

Darkness comes early in the afternoon in January. For many people on a late winter weekend afternoon, this was a time for warm fires, dinner with good friends, maybe a movie or a basketball game. For me, this January, it was a time for finding my way, trying to create a new life. The State of North Carolina had locked my physical self in prison. I had to keep them from getting the rest of me.

A narrow dirt track circled most of the yard below the dorms. It went past the basketball play area, by the canteen, and finally by one of the first dorms built here. Almost half the track was bordered by a large fence with curling barbed wire on top, meant to slice, not to cut, with signs posted that read "Do not come within four feet of the fence."

I met many of the inmates on my walks around this track. To complete one full circle, I went by benches and picnic tables where other men sat and passed the day away. They were either watching basketball games, waiting for a telephone to open up, or just sitting together, smoking cigarettes and staring vacantly ahead. I did notice one thing. Mostly blacks played basketball. When the whites joined them, they got creamed. Even in prison, white guys can't jump.

I need to tell you that I was not harmed in prison. My purpose was to survive and to get through my time there as best I could. If I could walk and talk to people, I did so. If someone asked me for advice on anything I knew about, I gave it. If someone just needed somebody else to talk to, I listened. I tried hard to care about the people I met in prison. The problem with too many of them is that no one, including themselves, ever has. They are forgotten until it is time to let them out.

Walking in an outside circle in a green prison uniform focused my mind. As I made my daily laps, the fence regularly reminded me that I was not free. At some point, on one of my laps, I stopped feeling sorry for myself. I talked to myself incessantly and urged myself on. I looked at everyone and everything. I wanted to see it all.

In the front of the prison were two tall flag poles, one holding the American flag, the other the state flag of North Carolina. I looked at them on every lap around the yard. Two symbols, representing the best of us, standing watch over what many considered to be the worst of us.

On the roadside beyond, cars went by. If a passenger in one of those cars had looked to the side that held the prison, he would have seen a tranquil place, a large grass lawn in front of a modern brick building holding the administrative offices of the prison. There was even a sign telling people thanks for coming and come back soon.

It looked all in order, everyone accounted for, made sure by four counts a day. Guards came and went on their eight-hour shifts, wearing their official blue uniforms. Every inmate going inside was patted down each time he entered. No one entered or left without being signed in or out.

But inside, not inside the fence but inside the minds and bodies of the inmates, was everything in order? Was the public being made safer by their incarceration? What would happen when some, or all of them, got out? Did anybody care?

As the days and then weeks went by, I became intrigued by Joe Spence. I decided I'd look up his case. He had been in prison most of his adult life, yet he seemed at peace with himself. I wanted to learn this from him if I could.

One day when I saw him I said, "Joe, you and I have to talk sometime."

"Okay, I'm here. I'll talk to you anytime you want. Just let me know."

"I looked up your case today at work." I'd checked the *North Carolina Supreme Court Reports*—a legal book that contains court opinions.

"You did, huh?"

"Yeah, you took up a whole lot of that book."

"Oh, I know it. Took up a lot of my life, too."

"When do you come up for parole again?"

"In May, but I don't think too much about it. I've been turned down so many times."

"How have you been able to live in here so long? I mean, really, how have you survived without losing your mind?"

"I've almost lost it, a number of times. You know, I've been in prison almost twenty-seven years, Jim. Think about it, almost twenty-seven years. My father died last year. I wanted to get out before he left us, but . . . I couldn't. So, I'm here."

"How's your mother? Is her health pretty good?"

"Well. She's seventy-six years old and has some problems getting around, but she's okay. I call her every morning, and, of course, I see her on weekends when I get a home pass."

"How long have you been getting home passes?"

"Four and a half years. No write-ups for eleven years. My co-defendant, who got the same sentence I got, and who shot the cab driver first and actually killed him, he got paroled last year. But they turned me down. They actually let him go and turned me down."

"That doesn't make sense."

"Doesn't make sense to you? It damn sure don't make sense to me."

"I just don't see how you've done it all these years, I really don't."

"Oh, well, sometimes I do better than at others."

"I wish I could do something to help you get out of here. You're no threat to anybody outside."

"Oh, I know, but tell that to the Parole Commission."

Walking back to my bunk that night, I thought about prison differently. Joe and I were in the same place. We slept not 20 feet apart. But I knew that I would not be inside long. Joe might very well die here. Though I'd made up my mind that I could handle prison and survive well, his situation made mine seem trivial. His crime was terrible. By his own admission, it had taken him seventeen years to transform himself from a killer into a decent man whom we could trust to not hurt us.

I talked to Senator Morgan about Joe and the senator did represent him, but Joe's still in prison. Hearing Joe talk about the hopelessness and loneliness of life, yet still retain kindness and a sense of humor, taught me much about the human spirit. Is rehabilitation possible? Should we execute everyone convicted of murder? When has someone paid a high enough price for committing a horrible crime? I don't know the answers to these questions. I only know that the man who helped take a life many years ago changed into someone who now had become a friend.

A short while later, Mr. Brown nodded to me to come to the front desk.

"Jim, did you go to Durham today?"

He was asking if I'd gone to therapy today. "Yep. Went over

this morning. Got to go again tomorrow night to my group session."

"Has that doctor helped you any?"

"Listen, Mr. Brown, she saved my life, it's that simple. May not be worth much now, but it sure wasn't worth a damn before she got hold of it."

"What do you mean?"

"It's like this. You've read in the paper all year that I took money and signed other people's names to court orders."

"Yeah."

"Dr. Spaulding helped get me through this. I see her because I need to. The hardest thing in the world is for me to tell you I have been clinically depressed, that I have suffered and continue to suffer from a mental illness. It's much easier for me to tell you that I took some money and I'm a criminal."

"I can understand that. People don't rightly know whether to believe you're sick or not, because you're not in bed."

"That's right. You know it's funny. Part of me blames people for being so narrow-minded, but part of me understands it perfectly because I used to be like that."

"Well, Jim, I have no doubt that if you stick to it, you can come back out on top again sometime. I hope so. Maybe this time in here will be good for you, let you rest some without people bothering you all the time to do something for them. Course, I've watched you in here. You can hardly get a moment's peace without someone asking you for some advice or help. I wouldn't let them get to me though."

"I understand."

"Jim, doesn't your basketball team play tonight?"

"Yeah, I'm afraid we do."

Wake Forest University was playing University of North Carolina at Chapel Hill. I've attended both schools, Wake Forest for undergraduate work and UNC-Chapel Hill for law school, but Wake Forest is my team. Dad was campus chaplain at Wake Forest University; my mother lives in a retirement center on campus at Wake; Marsha, Jeff, and Stacy have all attended Wake Forest. Yeah, they're my team.

"I thought so. But, you never know. They might give Carolina a run for their money."

"I can't watch it anymore. Gets me too upset. Think I'll go read."

"Okay. See you later."

The Wake-Carolina basketball game started at 9:00 P.M., which meant that by the second half the lights in the bunk area were turned off. Every few minutes, I heard a huge roar from the dayroom and knew that someone was doing well. Finally, I couldn't stand it any longer and got up to see who was winning. We were, though not by very much.

I walked back to bed, climbed up, and sat there. I couldn't sleep, but I didn't want to watch the game. So, I did what I always do. I got up and paced. As I was walking back and forth at the opposite end of the dorm, an inmate walked up to me and stared.

"Jim, are you all right? Are you sick or something? Have you gotten bad news?"

I looked back and smiled just a little. "Yeah, I'm okay. I'm just nervous about the game."

"You're nervous about a basketball game? Man, you're crazy. All that you've got on your mind, and you're concerned about a game? Man."

He was right, of course. But my pacing worked. We won the game.

My Recovery Takes Hold

With the beginning of March, the weather began to improve and weekends were spent outside as much as possible. Our thoughts turned to one thing—getting out of prison. Inmates rarely asked what another prisoner had done to get into prison, but they always wanted to know when someone was getting out.

I had settled in as much as possible. I ate my meals in the dining hall, talked to the other guys, gossiped with them about which guards were the best and the worst, stood outside and drank coffee and listened to the boom boxes. I'd learned that for three dollars a week I could have my laundry done, for one dollar my shoes shined and cleaned, and, if I asked the right person, I could get some new T-shirts and some pants with back pockets that weren't falling off.

I went to meetings of Alcoholics Anonymous, partly because I'd never been to a meeting, but also because it was good escape from the dorm. They also had free cake.

On two Saturday nights, I went to church services, which were held in the dining hall. The services always started with about a dozen hymns. I rarely knew the names of the songs, but it didn't matter. It was a place where people went to escape and to seek hope. It was not accidental that we always ended with the old favorite, "Amazing Grace."

March was a month of becoming friends with people I would never have met in any other way. My conversations with Joe continued as he patiently explained how he'd built a life with no freedom and no physical possessions beyond what he could cram into a small locker. I came to admire the man he'd made himself become.

Many nights, Joe's stories of life in Central Prison, a maximum facility, and Caledonia Farms, where he survived by being one of the meanest around, kept us going way past lights out.

I saw Ricky change from a relatively happy person to someone bitter about spending more time in prison than he felt he should. He was being forced to max out his sentence, despite a good work record and no write-ups about bad conduct. He had behaved himself and it had done him no good. He was a number in the system, and he had no one to fight for him.

I watched people come in after being convicted several times of driving while impaired. I hoped that once they were out they wouldn't do that again, but I didn't hold my breath on that. Too often, these people were not bad people. They simply could not keep away from alcohol. Did prison help them? I don't know, but perhaps some lives were saved while they were inside, including their own.

The Bible was the most read book in prison. Inmates didn't just read it, they studied it and answered questions that had been submitted to them about the Bible from various Bible study groups. They listened to gospel music and religious services on the radio. Were all these people sincere about what they were doing? I really have no idea. I do know that what they were all seeking was hope and an understanding of what to do with the rest of their lives.

Racism expressed itself in so many ways. One night, a loud noise erupted in the dorm. "Who's doing that?" I asked.

Ricky responded first. "He's one of our newest members. Probably not over twenty years old. Think's he's a dude, listening to his music, shaking up and down the room. He's happy to be here. Trying to show the older ones he can handle it."

"Why is he happy to be here?"

"Think about it. He gets a bed, warm place to sleep, three meals a day. Better than he's had it on the street."

"Look at his pants. They're about to fall off his tail."

"Oh, they all wear them like that now. Probably just to irritate us whites. If they can get down on us, then that's made their day."

"That's unbelievable." By now white kids wear their pants real low, too. Probably to irritate all adults, black and white

By this time, other inmates close by had wandered over to listen in on the conversation. One of them, a well-mannered white man in his mid to late forties from the L side of the dorm, spoke up. "There's no such thing as rehabilitation in prison, at least not in North Carolina. If you want rehabilitation, you do it yourself. Don't wait for anybody else. All they're going to do is warehouse you, that's it. After that, you're on your own."

Dwight agreed. "He's right. This place doesn't care about nothing except count time, making sure we're all here. They work their eight-hour shifts and they're gone."

"Good grief," I said. "And I thought I was depressed before I came in here. I need a drink."

Both blacks and whites practiced racism. The young blacks, for the most part, were insolent, rude, and almost certain to return to prison after being released. They had to prove to each other how tough they were, and how they didn't give a damn about the white man's world or law. They saw themselves as victims ruled by whites, who were clearly the enemy.

They saw the older blacks, those more quiet and behaved, as people who had given up and sold out to the white man. There was a quiet and unspoken, but very clear, hostility between the younger and older blacks.

For too many young people, entering prison resembled the beginning of school in the fall. Instead of questions like, "Which teacher did you get?" and "What did you do for your summer vacation?" it was "Which prison did you come from?" "How much time did you get?" "What dorm are you in?"

Whites were no better. The most frequent comment I heard was, "If you didn't like them before, you'll hate them when you leave." The whites were vastly outnumbered by the blacks in prison, almost four to one. So the whites grumbled to themselves and made sure they sat on the opposite side of the dining hall whenever possible. I never saw a black person and a white person listening to music together or spending much time talking together. Even the guards segregated themselves. The blacks kept to themselves, so did the whites.

But I was the only lawyer or ex-lawyer in the prison, black or white, which made me the only potential source of help. Besides that, I had no secrets. As one of the administrators told me, "Jim, there's not a person in this unit—staff, guards or inmates—who doesn't know who you are and why you're here. You are watched more closely than anyone else is, trust me on that. Some people want you to do well, and some would love to see you fail and fall on your face. You just have to accept that."

So, blacks as well as whites talked to me, and often. They were hungry for information about parole, their cases, their lawyers, judges, or creditors who were after their families.

During this time I learned to say no. Very little of what I could say was good news, but I told them just the same. If I could bring them something from work, like a reported appellate case, I did so. If I could help them write or type a letter, I did so. If I could refer them to a lawyer, I did so. They didn't ask for much, and they were always grateful for anything I could do, even the toughest inmates. A little help and kindness often turned a mean stare into "Hello, Mr. Blackburn."

It was in prison that I really learned that my life was not over.

I'd gone in literally with only the clothes on my back, and I didn't get to keep them for long. But I'd also gone in with the tremendous love and support of family and friends. I'd gone in with all I'd learned in my life, both the good and the bad.

I'd also gone in with frustration and anger, but I worked to put those emotions either aside or to better use. I had gone into prison to be punished, to pay a debt—to give my pound of flesh, whatever that was to be.

I walked into the darkest part of my life with no map, no knowledge of how to act. I could only treat people as I wished to be treated and hope that was enough. It was.

Few inmates were mean to me: The bearded man who never spoke to me except to insult me for being a prosecutor. His friend, who wound up replacing Smitty as my lower bunkmate, refused to shake my hand and tried to play mind games with me by telling everyone that I regularly had nightmares and pounded the locker next to me. The older man who always got up from my table in the dining hall when I sat down, because he wanted to show others that he wouldn't associate with anyone who had once been responsible for helping to send people to prison.

But they were far outnumbered by the men who called out to me as I walked in the yard, yelling, "Hey, Blackburn, my man"; the ones who told me they were praying for me or gave me Bible verses; the nurse who gave me jelly beans on Valentine's Day along with my regular medicine; the guards who told me how much they admired what I used to do; the many—guards and in-mates—who told me to take care of myself, that I didn't belong in prison, and to behave myself when I got out so that I didn't come back.

It was in prison that I finally learned to like and accept myself. This alone told me I'd made a significant leap in my recovery. During the year before, I wondered who I was because I was no longer a lawyer. I didn't think I had any identity separate from that. While I was now perhaps a jailhouse lawyer, I was finding out who I really was. I decided I liked Jim Blackburn.

False Spring

On a warm morning in early April, my hopes for the future were at their highest. George Sloan, my faithful friend and now driving companion, picked me up every morning in his old white Oldsmobile Cutlass to take me to Senator Morgan's office. George was a private detective in Raleigh who had worked with me for years in both domestic and criminal cases. He was short, well-built, had slightly graying hair, and was totally fearless.

We had just pulled left onto Rock Quarry Road. I suggested, "George, let's stop by Wendy's and get coffee to celebrate."

"Sounds like a winner to me. What are we celebrating?"

"The nurse called me into her office this morning and started asking me questions about my medicine for the future. I must have looked puzzled, because she soon told me my papers were up front, that they had come in yesterday."

"That's great. When does that mean you'll be released?"

"I don't know. I'll call my probation officer this morning to see what she knows. Maybe I can get out this week. I'll call you later today and let you know about picking me up the rest of the week."

"That's fine. I hope it's soon."

"Boy, so do I."

"You know what, George? This means I might get out in time for spring. I won't miss it after all. It's really been strange riding through these streets where I used to walk all the time, but now I can't. But maybe, pretty soon, I can again. People take so much for granted. Just walking and driving around. They think they'll do that forever. It's like a friend of mine who lives for the weekend. I used to do that. I don't think I ever will again. You better live each day."

"Jim, you sound serious today."

"I know, maybe I need another cup of coffee. Thanks for the ride. I'll talk to you later in the day."

I got out of the car and walked into the Capital Club Building, which housed a number of lawyers, including the law firm of Morgan and Reeves. I was early today, so I opened the office and made the coffee.

Within ten minutes, Senator Morgan walked through the door.

"Good morning, Blackburn. How are you doing today?"

"Not bad. I heard this morning that my parole papers are here. I might get out this week."

"Not if I can help it. I'm going to call the Parole Commission first thing and have your parole revoked. This is the first time in my life I've ever had a lawyer where I wanted him. You can't go anywhere. You have to stay here. I know you're here in the morning when I get here, and you're here when I leave, and when I call in from out of town. I sort of like it." He grinned at me and asked, "What are you going to do when you get out? Do you know yet?"

"I'll probably take a few days off. Then come on back here, if that's okay with you."

"I'm counting on your doing that."

"Good."

A few hours and telephone calls later, I learned I would be released the following morning at about 11 o'clock. My parole officer would come to the prison with a stack of necessary forms, we'd fill them out, and she'd take me home.

I was excited, but I wanted to take in all of my last day in prison. Strange as it may seem, that is where I wanted to eat dinner that night and visit with everyone. I wanted to say goodbye.

The next morning was sunny and warm. The azaleas next to the control center were in full white bloom. The grass had turned green, and I could smell the cut grass as some of my friends guided their lawnmowers over large patches of lawn.

I skipped breakfast but went down to the area where everyone waited for his ride to work. It was my last day, and I wanted one more visit with men who had treated me well when I needed it most. There were plenty of well wishes, and I left them with feelings of friendship.

I walked over to the canteen for coffee.

The man behind the counter said to me, "Jim, you've made the news again this morning. They say you're being paroled."

"Is that it?"

"Yeah, but I bet you the cameras will be here when you leave. Hell, you ought to go out the back way so they can't see you."

"No, I'll tell you, they were so anxious to take my picture and write about me going in, I want them there when I go out. If they weren't there, I'd call them to come."

I walked back to the dorm and slowly changed clothes. During my entire time in prison, I had never worn a tie. On occasion I had worn a tie at work, but I had changed into it there, never at prison. But today, my last day, I had brought a tie to wear out. I guess that was my protest and my shaking of the fist. I put it on and sat down to wait.

I had already given my valuables away to others. To Ricky, I gave my small mirror that had magnets on the back, good for hanging on locker doors and even the smoky mirrors in the bathroom. To Dwight Pruitt, I gave a lock, not the one Smitty gave me that didn't work, but one that another inmate had given me that did work. The lock was special to me. Three times I locked the keys in my locker and three times Ricky and Joe Spence got them out, every time within five minutes, using a broomstick and a coat hanger.

My coat hangers went to an inmate across the aisle, as did my sugar for coffee and the stirrers. My wooden shelf that Smitty had given me, along with the soft drink cans that held it up, went to my new lower bunkmate. He was recently married and had just come in on a drug possession charge.

Shortly after 11 A.M. a voice called my name over the loud-speaker and told me to go to the front office. I was excited.

I walked to the sergeant's office and got my bag of clothes. Then, I went through the dining hall to the administrative wing of the building. Kim McCauley, my parole officer, was waiting for me.

"Jim, the television people are here. They want to know if you will give them an interview. They even asked to be present while I go over this paperwork with you so they can film that."

I laughed. "You look nice today, Kim, and your hair's recently been done. You were expecting this, weren't you?"

"Jim, I've already gotten so much teasing about my hair at work this morning. When I made the appointment, I had no idea you'd be getting out today."

"Sure."

"Well, listen, what do you want to do about them?"

"Tell them after I'm out, they can ask me anything they want. But until then, no."

"Good."

After about an hour, we were through, and I had signed all the necessary parole forms. I saw that they were properly signed by members of the Parole Commission as well. It was time to go.

We walked through the dining hall so that we could leave through the prison entrance. Here, two locked gate doors had to be opened from the gate room. As the second one opened just a bit, I kicked it the rest of the way and walked out.

Reporters from two local television stations were there as well as a photographer from the local paper. I answered their questions and had my picture taken while other inmates looked on from a distance. I looked back one last time and waved to two of them who had lived in my dorm. They waved back, and I got inside Kim's car to leave prison, this time for good.

"Tell me the way to your house."

Gladly.

No one was home when we got there. Marsha had to work and Stacy was still in school, as was Jeff, who was at Wake Forest University in Winston-Salem, North Carolina.

Kim parked out front, and the two of us walked to the house. As we did, I saw a big yellow ribbon tied around an old oak tree in our yard. It was Wednesday, April 6, 1994. I had not been there since the cold afternoon of Monday, January 3.

Inside, as I walked through the kitchen and den, I saw everything as it once was. The furniture was in the same place. The daily newspaper was still kept on the top of the kitchen table. I tried to imagine what life had been like here the last three months. I felt distant and somewhat formal. I had grown comfortable on my top bunk in K and L Dorm and wasn't sure what to do.

Shortly, Kim left and told me to call her the next day. I went upstairs, took off my tie, and changed into slacks and a short-sleeved shirt. Within fifteen minutes, the doorbell rang, and it was Sheila Singleton. Charlie Hinton, Sheila, and I had arranged to have lunch at 42nd Street Oyster Bar.

While we waited for Charlie, I wandered around the inside of the house, realizing all the things it meant to be free. No more searches, no more pat downs, no more counts, and no more green clothes. I was free and out of prison.

Later that afternoon, after lunch, the three of us went to a place we nicknamed the "Little White House." We had started a nonprofit organization to educate people about clinical and manic depression, and this was our headquarters. It was an old house with peeling white paint. Its color was the only similarity to its cousin in Washington, D.C.

Sheila dropped me off at home at about 2:30 P.M. I wanted to be there when Stacy came home from school. As I walked into

Freedom aborted: I walk out the gate of Wake Correctional Center at noon thinking I'm a free man. Hours later I learn my release has been a mistake. I went back.

the upstairs bedroom, the telephone rang. Senator Morgan on the line. He sounded serious.

"Jim, have you talked to anyone since you got home?"

"No, why?"

"They're looking for you."

"Who's looking for me?"

"Correction people, the Parole Commission. There's been some kind of mistake. They say they shouldn't have released you today. Something about computation of the time."

"The hell you say."

"No, Jim, I'm serious. I'm not kidding. I've been on the telephone with the attorney general's office to see if they can go ahead and issue their ruling on that new statute that allows the commission to release nonviolent offenders early if there's an overcrowding problem, which there certainly is."

"What do you think I should do?"

"Just sit still for a few minutes. I'm still waiting for word on this. Don't answer the phone. I'll call and let it ring twice. Then, I'll call back again, and you'll know it's me. Then, we can decide what to do."

I put down the phone and slumped down in a chair. I put my right hand to my head and sat there for the longest time. I didn't want to open my eyes. Maybe if I kept them shut, this would all go away.

I didn't know what to do. But I knew what I did not want. I did not want to be free on a new statute, an exemption that would amount to special treatment. I did not go through all the pain and humiliation so I could hold my head up only to be denied an honorable end. That afternoon, without anyone telling me, I knew what I had to do. I would go back, and I would go back before they told me to do so.

Just then, I heard the dogs barking, which meant someone was at the door. I walked downstairs and saw my father walking in the back door.

"Jim, how are you doing?"

"I'm doing okay."

"I don't know whether you are or not."

"I don't either, but I'll be fine." I walked outside and saw that Marsha had just driven into the garage and was lifting groceries out of the trunk.

"Hi, honey, welcome home."

"Thanks. We have a small problem. They claim they made a mistake, and I shouldn't have been released today. I may have to go back."

"Oh, no."

"Yeah. Dad's inside. I don't really want to talk to anyone now."

"I understand. What do we do?"

"Robert's going to call me back soon, and then we'll know what's happening."

We walked back inside. I went upstairs just as the phone rang. I waited. Two rings, then nothing. Then, another ring. I picked up the phone.

"Jim, I still don't know anything. I haven't heard back from anyone," Senator Morgan said.

"Robert, I don't think you'll hear anything on me this afternoon. No one wants to touch this."

"You may be right."

"I know what I need to do. I want to go back to prison now. Then, whatever happens can happen. But I want to be there, not here, when it does."

"I think you're right."

"I'll talk with you soon."

Marsha walked into the bedroom.

"I just talked to Robert. I think I need to go back to prison now. Can you take me?"

"Yes, but Betsy and Adrienne just drove up, with supper for tonight. What do you want me to do about that?"

Betsy Hinton (Charlie's wife) and Adrienne Clark are two of our closest friends. "Take it and you can eat it later tonight," I said. "But I'm going back right away."

Downstairs, I told my father I'd talk with him later. Outside, Betsy and Adrienne held the food they'd cooked for a supper to welcome me home. I walked over to Betsy.

"I'm sorry I can't stay. It smells good."

"Jim, this is awful, just awful."

"Well, that's true, but I can't do anything about it. I've got to go back. Thanks for coming over, though." I was trying to remain calm.

Just then, Stacy, home from soccer practice at school, bounded out of a car and across the front yard. She was smiling and happy as she did so.

"Welcome home, Daddy. It's good to see you."

"Stacy, there's been a mistake. I have to go back now. Why don't you get in the car and go with us."

She looked at me as if I was telling her a sick joke. But it quickly dawned on her that this was no joke and I was leaving then, with or without her. She got in the car.

Marsha drove. Stacy sat in the back seat. It was not a happy ride, but both Marsha and I felt that I was doing the right thing at the right time.

"Look at it this way, Jim, this is another chapter for your book."

For a long time, I had thought about writing a book about this. We all sort of joked about it but I did make notes. It was also a way of speaking about this situation.

"I'm tired of gaining new chapters for my book. I want it to end."

We turned into the prison driveway. The news cameras were there. Five uniformed guards stood at the gate that I had kicked open just hours before.

I turned to Marsha and said, "Just turn around. I'll jump out of the car and you can go. Don't park the car."

Before I could open the door, the camera was staring at me through the window. I got out and Marsha sped away. It was the Durham television station camera. The reporter asking questions was Dave Bolick, who had written about some of my previous cases and had followed me in this story. He had interviewed me on my release earlier that day.

"Jim, this is unbelievable. How do you feel?"

"I'm okay, Dave."

"This must be quite a shock to you. How did you hear?"

"Robert Morgan told me, just a little while ago."

"What was freedom like for you—the hours you had?"

"Well, I had a good lunch. Talked to some friends. But when I learned there was a problem, I came back. If someone has made a mistake, and we all do, then I want to do what's right, if I can."

"What do you do now?"

"Get my old bunk back, I hope. That's my biggest concern. I may pass on supper here, though. I'm not ready to walk back into the dining hall."

"Thanks, Jim."

"You're welcome, Dave."

I started to walk away. The cameras were still on but the mike was off. Dave walked over to me and shook my hand. He looked at me, smiled, and said, "Jim, you're a hell of a guy."

I nodded and turned around and walked to the gate. It opened electronically. I didn't know why so many guards were there and whether they were going to frisk me or what. What they did was gather around me, shake my hand, and welcome me back. There was no frisk this time.

I walked past the weight pile, the control center, and down by the telephone bank. The inmates just stood there and watched. No one spoke, not a word. It was the quietest I ever saw the place during the daytime.

I looked ahead and saw Ike walking towards me. Ike was an inmate who was in charge of the laundry. He often visited in our dorm.

"Ike?"

"Hey, man, I heard what happened to you. That really stinks."

"Thanks. I need your help. I don't have any bed stuff left. I turned it all in this morning before I left. Can I come back to the clothes room with you in a minute and get what I need?"

"No. Tell you what. I'll get it for you and bring it up to you in a few minutes."

The sergeant said to me, "You can have your old bunk back, if you want it."

"Thanks, I do."

I walked back into K and L Dorm and saw my empty bunk. Lying on top was my mirror and lock. Ricky and Dwight had put them back for me. Also, on the pillow was everything else that I had given away that morning. The stirrers, packets of sugar, the shelf, even the drink cans to hold up the shelf were there. I opened the locker and looked inside. Empty. It had been full of life days before. Now, no books, no coffee, no letters from friends, no clothes, clean or otherwise. Just empty.

I'd had four hours of freedom, and now I felt empty. I had to start over. I had worked very hard to adapt to prison and to accept the limited life that was imprisonment. Through it all—the indictment, plea, sentencing, entry into prison, searches of myself and my locker, no privacy—I had somehow endured and survived. I had even become a stronger and better person, I told myself. Oh, every step had thrown me and thown me hard. But nothing, *nothing,* was like this.

I climbed up on top of my mattress, which sank in the middle, and lay there with my eyes closed. I didn't want to go anywhere or talk to anyone. I didn't want anyone to be nice to me. I wanted to be left alone.

Perhaps in January, I could have been left alone, but not in April. Even though I had been there only three months, that was enough time for friendships to form. No one would leave me alone, not just in my dorm, but throughout the prison.

In the blink of an eye, I had become a victim of the system, much as the other inmates imagined themselves to be. That night, Mr. Brown, the dorm guard, came to me and put his hand on my lower leg and asked me if I wanted to share the ribs his wife had made.

At about 8:00 P.M., Kim McCauley came back to the prison and asked permission to visit with me. We did so, with a number of the officers, in the control center. I sat on the floor. The next morning, a black inmate I'd seen at the church services came up to me, shook my hand, and handed me a piece of paper.

"James, I'm praying for you, brother. I'm praying for you."

I opened the paper and saw that it had Bible verses written on it, with the notation, "To my brother, James."

That same morning, Cecil Hicks came up to me with a cup of freshly brewed coffee. A mild-mannered fellow who had a serious drunk-driving record, Cecil was a hard worker at the control center. He was scheduled for release in May.

"Mr. Blackburn, if you'll see me each morning, I'll be sure to get you a cup. You don't have to ask. When I see you, I'll get it for you."

Later that morning, I met with the unit superintendent and another officer. They told me that my work release and level at the prison were set. I would spend the rest of the month in prison. Everyone was trying to make the best of it for me after the mistake of the day before.

I walked outside and saw Joe Spence, who hadn't spoken to me the night before. "Hello, Joe."

"Hey, Jim, how are you this morning?"

"I've been better. How are you?"

"I'm okay. I thought you needed a little space, so I left you alone."

"I noticed."

"Listen, Jim. I know you're down. Maybe you have a right to be. But stop it. Don't you start feeling sorry for yourself. I've watched you since you came in. You've made a lot of progress; you can't let this throw you back. If you have to spend the rest of April in here, then spend it. You can do that. You know you can. But don't whine. You haven't whined yet. Don't start now."

"Joe, did anybody ever tell you that you have a hell of a bed-side manner?"

He started laughing. "Well, Jim, it isn't that I care so much about you. But you're the only lawyer, or ex-lawyer, I know. I've put too much effort into making you well and getting you through this to give up now. You're my only hope to my some day getting out of here. I want you to help me when you get out."

"And I thought you were getting soft on me."

"Jim, I've been here a long time, but not that long."

Freedom

Later that morning, I laughed when I saw my ride to work. Eric Reeves, Robert's law partner and son-in-law, picked me up in his Beetle convertible with the top down. It fit my mood perfectly, and the two of us drove into town laughing and listening to the radio. I wasn't all that happy. I was numb, and I didn't know what else to do than laugh.

Later that day, I walked upstairs to the twelfth floor to the Raleigh offices and studio for Channel 11, the Durham television station. I wanted to know the news about me and I knew that reporters often knew happenings before anyone else. They kindly put me in a room and let me watch the clips for the evening newscast to be broadcast later that night. The people being interviewed were kind to me and said they regretted the mistaken early release.

So at the end of the day, I still went back to prison while everyone else went home. Marsha went to the beach. Originally, I was going to stay at home with Stacy.

That weekend, the sun was out and the guards opened a gate to a lower softball field so inmates could play kickball. It was about 10:30 on Sunday morning when I walked over to the metal bleachers behind the screen near home plate. I looked around, took off my shirt, rolled my pants legs up and lay down to get a suntan. I lay there for about an hour before it was time for lunch, easily the culinary high point of the week.

It seemed a simple thing then, but looking back, it is so remarkable to me that I felt that comfortable in prison that day to lie down behind home plate and sunbathe. In its own small way, it is a measure of how far I had come. I was relaxed that day. I wasn't overjoyed to be back, but I was at peace with myself for coming back without being ordered back. When I mentioned the sunbathing incident to a friend, she said, "Well, why shouldn't you do that? After all, it is the same sun that we have."

As the real end of my imprisonment neared, I wondered what life outside would be like. How would people react to me? I wondered whether I would face prejudice in the future not only because of the criminal charges that had landed me in prison, but also because of the widespread publicity of my clinical depression, but I felt that a lot of that depended on me. I knew that I must not hide.

Senator Morgan made my readmission to the world possible. He made me go places with him. He took me everywhere from the courthouse to the police station, for lunch at the City Club to lawyers' offices, and anywhere else he could imagine. He included me in meetings with his clients and visitors. He was there at the beginning for me, and he was there at the end.

I'll never forget when Dr. Jean Spaulding's oldest daughter asked her, "How is Jim doing? Does he know yet what it is to be black?"

I was startled by the question. No one had ever asked me anything like that. But then, I had never been this different before. I'd never been forced to ride at the back of the bus, but the people back there are as good as those at the front. There is no real difference. That lesson alone was worth the price of the ticket.

I learned what it was like to be different, to be convicted of criminal wrongdoing and become an inmate. I learned what it was like to be diagnosed with severe clinical depression and to take antidepressant medication. I learned what it was like to be treated differently because of these events. That is what was meant by, "Does he know yet what it is to be black?"

I spent my last morning in prison in K and L Dorm, sitting on a bed and talking to a black dorm officer, a man I'd been warned held the strongest prejudice against whites of all the African-Americans in the unit. More than once I'd heard, "Don't talk to him. He's looking to hurt you because you're white."

Our conversation that morning? He was a deacon at a Baptist church in northern Wake County. His church had grown by the hundreds over the last two years. He was telling me why. It wasn't racism. It was faith.

Basically, I learned that all people, black and white, those in prison and out, all want the same things: We want to be healthy and secure. We want our families to be happy. We want to be happy. Unfortunately, not all of us know how to accomplish these things. Fortunately, God is patient with us. He knows, even if some of us don't, that it is the same sun that watches over us all.

If ever I doubt that again, I only have to close my eyes and remember the words "Mr. Blackburn, thank you . . . Jim, can you help me . . . If you ever need me to do anything for you, let me know . . . When you get out, I want you to come to my house for dinner . . . I wish you good luck . . . I've been praying for you, brother James . . . Please don't forget me when you get out, and I'm still here"

At midafternoon, twenty days after the first time, I left prison again. But I will really never leave. For it is, and always will be, a part of who I am.

I'd seen the Neil Simon movie, *Chapter Two,* about starting over. I was ready, that spring day, to begin my own Chapter Two—My Recovery from Flame-out. I had to wonder as we drove away from prison this second time, whether God had always known how this would turn out. As I sat in the front passenger's seat again and rode home to freedom, I leaned back, closed my eyes and whispered, "Thanks, God."

I swear I heard a voice whisper back, "You're welcome."

42nd Street Oyster Bar

I wish I could explain why a seafood restaurant in Raleigh became special to me. The 42nd Street Oyster Bar was once a small corner place designed as a hangout for friends back during the late years of prohibition. Named after 42nd Street in New York City, it was home to locals and college students until it closed in 1974.

The restaurant was resurrected in the late 1980s at the same general location, but as a much larger and grander seafood restaurant with an emphasis on oysters, anyway you liked them.

For many years, I had been a frequent customer at the 42nd Street Oyster Bar. It was an easy three-block walk from my law office to the white cinderblock building with no windows. Near the entrance is a long oyster bar, beyond this dark wooden tables and booths fill a raised dining room. I used to lunch with law associates or casual friends there, away from the practice of law.

The Oyster Bar specializes in quick-service lunches that feature either a fresh fish of the day, an oyster or shrimp sandwich, or any sampling of fried food, all designed to make you feel like you're at the coast. Favored Oyster Bar dishes are oyster stew and a cheese potato, which is twice-baked mashed potatoes with a little onion mixed in and topped with cheddar.

My lunches there became more frequent as I decided it was my place to be. Over time, I started going there for a beer or two after work as well, as it became a Raleigh hotspot to meet other lawyers, bankers, and business people after work. Eventually, the Oyster Bar became a home away from home for me, and I found that my car had a difficult time driving by after work without stopping.

So in 1995, when I was trying to decide where to earn extra money and work outside the protective cocoon of Robert Morgan's law office, I thought of the Oyster Bar.

I spoke to the owner Brad Hurley and we arranged that I'd start on a Monday evening as a host, for beginning wages of only $6.00 per hour. Then I changed my mind. I wrote Brad a letter and laid it on his desk, saying that I could not do this. I could not bring myself to be a host at the very restaurant where I'd so often dined. People that I knew, for God's sake, might see me, and how demeaning would that be? So I quit before I even began.

Two days later, I changed my mind and asked for my job back. Brad agreed as long as I started in two hours. He didn't want to give me time to change my mind again.

Brad asked me to wear a coat and tie as opposed to the waiter's uniform of black polyester pants, white shirt, red suspenders, and red bow tie. I don't know whether he had a problem with seeing an older man dressed in the restaurant uniform or not. I rather suspect he hoped, as he said, that some guest might mistake me for someone important and make all his complaints to me rather than to him. Brad was smart that way.

At first, it was awkward. I walked with customers to their table or booth, laid the menus down, and told them to enjoy their meal. That part was easy. Walking back to the host station was not. For on the way back, I saw everyone in the restaurant and, by now, everyone had seen me. Members of the wait staff that I had known before looked at me in disbelief. As did the customers. But, like everything else in life, after the shock of what I was doing wore off in about half an hour, I started to relax and enjoy myself.

On that first night, someone standing next to me spilled a

drink on the floor, and after looking around to see who was going to clean it up, I realized that was my job. No one else was going to do it. But cleaning the floor of a restaurant while wearing a coat and tie seemed stupid to me. So the coat came off, and I began to feel much more at home. At the end of the night my manager told me she thought I had done a good job.

I worked there at least five nights a week. As the weeks went by, I relaxed with the customers and bantered easily with them as I took them to their tables. I only made a few miscues. One night, when I was feeling somewhat frisky, I was taking a lady and her husband to their table when—I don't know why—I asked when her baby was due. She looked at me in disbelief and told me she was not pregnant. Not to be outdone, I gently but firmly informed her that there would be "no more hushpuppies for you." I will always be grateful that both she and her husband laughed rather than decking me onto the floor.

The only time I remember a guest being nervous when I was hosting was one weekend night. I noticed a reservation made in the name of "Carolyn Hunt" and the request was for two people. Sure enough, at the appointed hour, Governor and Mrs. Hunt appeared at the entrance to the restaurant and inquired about their reservation for the evening. I looked up, saw who it was, and said "Hello, Governor."

Looking a little startled, the governor looked back and said, "Hello, Jim."

That was it. You would have thought he had seen a ghost—or at least someone with a camera who might take his picture with me. I quickly walked them to their table, sat them down, asked a question or two about how they were doing, and left them alone. He looked grateful for that.

Thinking back on both these occasions, I decided I was ready for the big time. If I could survive the embarrassment of insulting a customer and meeting the Governor and his wife as a host of a restaurant all in several weeks' time, perhaps I could do more than work for $6.00 per hour.

When you go to a restaurant and meet the host or hostess, re-member: this person makes no money. Truthfully, no one in the restaurant makes much money except the owner, and he will tell you he is the one who has to take the risks.

But in the feudal hierarchy of a restaurant staff, the position of waitperson is what you want. They are the ones who make the cash each night. They are also the ones who take the abuse that some customers, for whatever reason, feel they must inflict upon those they believe are in a lower station in life.

I asked for permission to train as a waiter. The assistant man-ager, Keith Nye, a rather large fellow with a friendly smile and hair cut in a flat top, said, "I have no problem with that. We can start you training next week. But, Jim, are you sure you will feel comfortable wearing the dress uniform we have here?"

"Keith, I wore prison greens for all those months. I guess I can wear whatever you have here."

He laughed and my career was born.

I must tell you that decision took some nerve on my part. I know that if you go into any restaurant in America, you will see hosts at the front door to greet you, a wait staff to serve you, and kitchen people who cook the food. It should not take a lot of courage to apply for these jobs. College kids do it every day of the year.

But when you have been a high-profile lawyer in town, have a lot of gray hair, and haven't been a college student in quite some time, I can tell you that it takes the traits of courage, humility, and the willingness to make a complete fool of yourself.

No one was very happy with me about my decision to do this. My doctor and lawyers felt I should not be at the restaurant so much, the very place I had frequented years earlier as a customer. I had never waited tables before, I would be working with younger people, and I'd be around all that money.

But Wade had said for a long time that I needed to work in the public sector where I was seen as doing nonlawyer work. He meant he wanted people to see me humbled and doing menial work. That way, I could do penance for my wrongdoing, which at some point might allow my return to society.

But I didn't seek to become a waiter for any of those reasons. I did it because I needed to make money, and Brad and Keith gave me a job. Waiting tables is not menial work, but it is hard. You have to be nice to all customers, regardless of whether they are nice to you. In fact, the worse a customer's behavior is, the more polite you try to be so that they'll leave happy enough to not stiff you.

You have to be gracious when you're tired and would rather be anywhere else. You have to smile and tell customers the specials as though they were sent from the gods, when in reality you wouldn't touch the stuff. You have to put up with ladies at lunch who order exactly the same thing, soup and salad, then ask for separate checks, each paying you with a twenty dollar bill. Then, at the very last minute, one of them wants hot tea. And always there is the husband and father, who orders first for himself, never thinking of his wife and child, who are left to fend for themselves. And finally there is prom night, when the girls come in dressed up in their gowns, and their dates don't have a clue as to how to act, what to order, and certainly don't have enough money left over to tip. If you are lucky, the girl has her father's credit card.

But all of this was in the future as I started to train. My first training session was at lunchtime. I followed the waitress around as she took everyone's order. I was introduced as a trainee at each table, and on occasion I was dispatched to get drinks for the customers, which usually consisted of either water or iced tea.

I thought I was doing pretty decently. But my trainer told me I was to stand up straight, never put my hands on the chairs at the table, and never, never put my foot on the lower rungs of the chairs.

At noon, it happened. At least twenty women from state government came to lunch. It was my worst nightmare. They were in a hurry and had to be back at work within an hour. They all wanted separate checks, and almost all of them paid with a twenty dollar bill. But making change for them was a small problem compared to the explanation I had to give the lady in a white blouse about how cocktail sauce happened to be dribbling down her backside. I quickly learned the value of soda water.

Timing is everything in being a waiter. People want to have their salads before their meals, not after. People want their water or tea refills before you have walked away from the table the first time. And they want their check when they want it, not before or after.

Most wait staff train for about four to five days, tops, before they are cut loose on an unsuspecting public. For me, it took about a month. How would you like to be described by a fellow human as *not* being "wait staff material"?

But I didn't quit, and no one asked me to. The only hint of concern I ever got was owner Brad Hurley's frequently repeated remark that whenever I was working, he often wanted to lie down in the office and rest a little.

I remember one lunch that one of the managers, Chris Morgan, a lanky dark-haired man, prefers to keep to himself.

It had been some time since my table had ordered and their food had not yet come up. They waved me over and told me they didn't have much time and politely asked if I could check on it. They had only ordered fried shrimp, which was one of the quickest items to cook.

I quickly went to the front line and looked at all the tickets. "Chris, there's no ticket here for table 113. They've been waiting for a long time. It's just fried shrimp."

Chris looked over the tickets carefully and agreed it wasn't up there waiting to be sold. He thought for a moment and asked, "Jim, are you sure you rang it in?"

"Chris, do you think I'm stupid? Of course I rang it in. Here, I'll show you." I went to the computer, opened the check to table 113, and all the check showed were two iced teas. No fried shrimp.

"Uh, Chris, guess what?"

Chris didn't hesitate. "Chef, two fried shrimp plates, on the fly. Jim forgot to ring them in."

"Thanks, Chris."

And then there were the lemons and the oranges. We cut up a lot of lemons each day for iced tea and to garnish the seafood. The first time I did it, I cut up almost an entire box of oranges before someone gently explained to me that it was lemons I should be doing. You know, the ones that are yellow? The chef, a short man from New York with a temper just as short, glared at me and muttered, "Oh well, I guess it's a good learning experience."

The learning curve for waiting tables is different from practicing law. Indeed, during one of my training sessions, another waiter once yelled at me, "Jim, your problem is that you are a lawyer. You think like one. Everything has to be thought over and analyzed. Forget you were ever a lawyer and just do it."

That was good advice and following it started my journey toward becoming a good waiter. I stopped worrying about my uniform and how I looked. I stopped worrying about what my friends would think when they saw me there. Most of them were happy to see me if only to ask if I could get them a good table. I concentrated on becoming a good waiter, making the most money I could, and learning to have a good time.

Waiting tables is a lot like trying a case before a jury. You get to speak first, and the customers have to listen. Some are attentive, some could care less. Some are very polite, and some give rudeness a bad name. The great unwashed public. If you can please them on a regular basis, you can do anything.

I really did learn to be a good waiter. I learned to take orders correctly, ring in the food on time, carry plates on my arm without dropping them, keep my sense of humor, answer questions about what fresh seafood we had that night, and, in the same breath, tell the customers why I believed Jeffrey MacDonald was guilty beyond a reasonable doubt. That question was asked at least as often as any other.

I learned to be on time, not put things off, and to enjoy myself. I learned about all the traits of survivorship that are so important. I learned anew that people want you to succeed even if you have made mistakes in the past. Indeed, that is when they want you to succeed the most. But if you don't try, you don't learn that.

If you ever have to start over at anything, I suggest you get around young people. First of all, many of them don't read the paper or listen to the news, and so they may not know who you are or why you are there. But if they do, they are often the most understanding people in the world. At least it was that way for me.

I became the uncle of the wait staff. I was easily the oldest one there. Most knew I had been a lawyer. Some of the older ones asked me about the MacDonald case, and the younger ones asked who Jeffrey MacDonald was.

I drank with them, laughed with them, stayed up late with them, and often closed the place down with them. There was Lorraine, twenty-seven years old, who was finishing school in Raleigh at North Carolina State University. She wanted to be a social worker. Lorraine was taller than me and often took my customer's bill from the computer and kissed it, so that it would have lipstick on it when I took it to the table—causing all kinds of looks. One night during the middle of a shift, we once danced. I dipped her and accidentally dropped her on the floor.

There was Sue, twenty-five years old and the mother of a young daughter. She was from Massachusetts and talked like it. She could drink with the best of them, once doing cartwheels at 2:00 A.M. on the Oyster Bar floor after drinking way too many shots.

There was Lee Ann, who was hopelessly in love with a guy back home in Nags Head and once, after too many drinks, took my hand, raised it upward, and asked me to close my eyes in a ten-second prayer for her and her boyfriend. The prayer didn't take, or perhaps God heard it and decided something else was best for Lee Ann.

There was Eleanor, the hostess, who always agreed with whatever I said, and who always tried to seat folks at my tables so I could make some money.

And Rhonda, who wanted to be a professional singer and actress. Once, at my request, she went to one of my tables and sang a song from Carousel because the customers were going to see that play later in the evening. I learned to have no shame. Anything for a good tip.

And Christine, who loved criminal law and crime novels and thought I should write one. She always made fun of my southern accent. But Christine is tough. She has two children, and just hours after the birth of her second child, she was back tending bar at the restaurant.

Mister Sam is from Africa via New York City. He has worked all his life, put three children through college, is proud and independent, and is married to a wonderful lady named Miss Maggie who makes the best soups in the world. One of my proudest moments was to be invited to their church for Sunday services at the dedication of their new sanctuary.

And there are others. Farelle, just twenty-three, blonde hair, almost always happy, and generally ready to share something to eat in the middle of a shift. Allan Brown, who constantly says, "There has to be another way to make money." Anita, the strikingly pretty bartender with long dark hair, who works the front bar. She knew me in my past life as a lawyer and wanted to visit me in Duke Hospital on the last Saturday I was there. She always laughed when she saw me in uniform.

I didn't have to work at fitting in. Once I decided to enjoy myself, I did fit in. I stopped worrying about who I was in the past. I thought more about who I was now. I didn't go to work living for hump day on Wednesday or the weekend, and the only reason I dreaded Monday was because it was the slowest night of the week and my chances for making one hundred dollars that day were not good.

I learned to live for the moment, or at least the hour that each of my customers were there. I did all that I could to make them happy, and when they left I usually had no regrets, particularly if they tipped me at twenty percent. But if they were cheap and left less than fifteen percent, I just looked forward to the next table. That is how waitpersons survive. We do the best we can while we are at work, and then we don't take it home with us.

I couldn't pretend, as I had once done in the practice of law. The customers either had their food, or they didn't. It was either fresh and hot, or cold and they'd ask, "Could you please take this back?"

I think all adults, especially lawyers, should have to wait tables at some point in their lives. Certainly it is just as essential to being a good lawyer or doctor or any professional or businessperson as it is to learn that profession or trade. You learn manners, how not to over-promise, how to deliver what you do promise, how to be on time, and how to enjoy each day and what you have. Waiting tables is not designed to teach a person these attributes; it just happens, whether you want it to or not. I wish I had learned such things years ago.

Some people came to 42nd Street Oyster Bar just to see if I was really working there. They were curious. They told me so. Others whispered about me as I went past their tables. Others would stop me, regardless of whether I was serving them, and tell me how much they admired me for what I was doing. One told me I was a wonderful role model for young people. Another, a total stranger, pressed a one hundred dollar bill in my hand, as did a former FBI agent from Charlotte who had been one of the foremost polygraph examiners in the Southeast.

I got hugs and handshakes from so many. People would stop

and ask me about the MacDonald case and whether I truly believed he was guilty and why did he do it. People would ask me how my own health was and tell me that someone they knew had once suffered from severe depression.

And sometimes I got stares and people clearly were amazed that I was there. I always had to live with my past. One of the managers once opened the cash drawer where I was ringing up a ticket. He had to leave for a moment. Before he did, he looked at me, smiled, and asked if he could trust me with the drawer open. I smiled back and told him to suit himself.

Most of all, I got friendship from the others who worked there. Whenever I was in too good a mood, several of them would call out that Jim was "off his drugs again or on too many," they weren't sure. Others would tease me about what they termed "sympathy tips," which as far as I know, spend the same as regular tips.

I'd stay late sometimes and drink wine with everyone after work. There is a ritual to working at a restaurant. After the night is over, you stay around awhile, order a glass of wine or a beer, and commiserate with each other about how little money you made, how the restaurant is going to hell in a handbasket, what terrible customers we had tonight, how the managers stand around with their hands in their pockets doing nothing, how we always run out of everything right in the middle of the evening, and how we all need to find another job.

But most of us come back the next night and the night after that. It is what we do. And we actually enjoy it. For a while, it becomes our life, and the highs and lows come every day.

You learn to share. You learn to help others. You do learn to be humble. If you hope to be successful at waiting tables, you learn to be optimistic and to make friends quickly. You learn that helping other people can make you happy. And perhaps most importantly, you learn that what you are doing is important. Someone else can take your job, but they cannot take your place.

Several years ago on Mother's Day, a terrible fire in a fraternity house at UNC-Chapel Hill took the life of the only son of two good friends. A few weeks later, on Father's Day weekend, they came to the Oyster Bar for dinner. I saw them and asked to wait on them. I asked Bonnie how she was doing.

"Not too well. It's still so new. It's only been five weeks. But I'm getting there."

"I know."

Well, of course, I didn't know. I really had no idea at all what it was like to lose a child. All I could do during the course of the evening was to make their time as pleasant as possible. I admired their grace and courage in making sure that I knew they were glad to see me.

In times of tragedy, we send food. That night was no different. Bonnie had told Brad that she wanted blackened grouper and oysters for dinner. Unfortunately, we had no such combination. So, he whispered to me to send her some complimentary fried oysters before her dinner of blackened grouper arrived.

Three of the four people at their table decided they wanted a glass of wine, so they asked to order a bottle of a new brand that we were featuring. Before I could enter the order, a waitress walked up to me and said quietly that a person at one of her tables wanted to purchase the bottle of wine for them.

At the end of the evening, no one wanted dessert, so I brought them one piece of bourbon pecan pie with vanilla ice cream and four forks. It was on me. Somehow it made me feel better. That I was, in some small way, participating in the recovery of their lives.

I think they had a good time at dinner. But, when it was over, they still had no son and had to go home to an empty house. But in the small step of venturing out, they had sent a sign that they were alive and trying to go on. Life is like that. When you are knocked down, you have to get up. It isn't fun, and it isn't easy. Some days, just getting up in the morning and putting one foot in front of the other becomes a challenge.

Several minutes later, a young couple came up to me and

spoke. They couldn't have been over twenty-five years old. They were pushing their infant in a stroller. I had waited on them a few weeks back when the mother was still expecting, and they just wanted to say hello.

Over at another table, I saw Dr. Annie Wilkerson, still strong but walking with a cane, now retired but for many years the best OB-GYN in town. She was supposed to have delivered my son Jeff when he was born and was present at the birth of my daughter, Stacy, four years later.

So in one night at the restaurant, I saw all of life, at its finest really. A young couple, freshly together with their baby; another couple, together in their grief over the unbelievable loss of a son, yet still able to smile gently and laugh; and a feisty baby doctor, who had been around long enough to have delivered us all.

As my friend Pete Carruthers would have noted, Bonnie and her husband, Leon, were broken and being honest about it. They were also showing us how to live—simply by continuing to live—the way they taught their son, with grace and courage. It is a lesson I am sure Dr. Annie knows well. It is one that the young couple will surely learn.

A long time ago, my father preached a sermon titled "The Joy of Serving." It was about Andrew, his brother Peter, and their relationship with Jesus. It was the younger Peter who became the star and perhaps the first disciple. No one really knew Andrew. But Andrew never faltered because of this lack of attention; he stayed with Jesus and did whatever he was asked. If he was needed to seat people at a gathering, he did it. He didn't have to be at the forefront. He was just happy to serve. He was there for the joy of it.

Waiting on other people gave me more than I could ever have guessed. It gave me my life back. I felt a level of happiness and satisfaction that I had not known in a long while. I remember the question Dr. Spaulding put to me early in my sessions with her: "What do you remember in black and white, and what do you remember in Technicolor?"

For me, the answer came after falling down and getting back up. It came after practicing law, hospitalization, inprisonment, and waiting tables. It came when and where I least expected. It came when I finally learned "The Joy of Serving."

Beyond MacDonald: Surviving Flame-out

At the beginning of this book, I mentioned a number of traits a person needs to survive and overcome adversity. I've thought about this a number of times from different perspectives. You might view these traits as necessary to avoid ruining the rest of your life or to keep you on a straight and narrow path. But perhaps these ideas, none of which are my own, represent simply the best way to live your life as you go through the inevitable turns that you will face on your own journey.

They worked for me. The trick is to keep following them. The danger is that as soon as we are doing better or the immediate adversity has passed, we go back to our old behaviors. At least that is what I tend to do. You may be different. But if not, this may be the best part of the book. These are the lessons I learned.

Develop a close relationship with God. Learn how to pray and talk regularly with God. This takes time because at first you pray with the wrong motivations. First, you pray to get out of your adverse situation. This will not work. Like it or not, you have to go through the bad time, and you are going to need some company along the way. This must be someone you can trust, someone who will not be judgmental, someone who loves you uncon-

Marsha and me, about eight weeks after I got out of prison. This is what freedom looks like.

ditionally. Not many people are like that. So, you should think about God.

Building this relationship is easier than you think. You have been taught all your life how to do this. It's just that you may not have done so with God. We tend to take God for granted, as though He will always be there. And of course He is.

The next thing you'll try is bargaining. That's what I did. Forget it. Didn't work. And you try to attach conditions. Won't work. Been there too. Forget it. Only when you surrender and tell God that He wins will you begin to make any progress.

This is what you pray for: The strength and courage to get

through the bad time That God's will, whatever that is, will be done. This sounds easy, but it is not. The problem is, God's will may well be different from yours.

You must keep this same prayer going all the time, regardless of what happens, and not give in to your normal selfish desire, which is to somehow get out of the mess easily and quickly.

What you don't realize at first is that the adversity itself will ultimately save you and give you your life back—but only if you are willing to deal with it. There are no shortcuts. The only way out is through. It will be hard and tough. At that point, God is probably the only game in town.

Learn to be humble. Embrace it. Be yourself. Learn to be like Andrew—do whatever is necessary to help others without the recompense of attention or profit. When you are willing to do the least important task, and be the best at it, is when you are the closest to being truly successful.

The good news about being humble is that people love humility. And so they will love you. The reason is simple—you are at your best. The irony in learning humility is that you get a head start on everyone else.

Anger is good. At times I was angry but I didn't want anyone to know. I held my feelings inside and appeared as though I was in control. Or so I assumed. Some people thought that I didn't care, others worried that I was wound so tightly I might explode. It was only when I got really angry in group therapy sessions that Dr. Jean Spaulding began to hope that I might get well.

It isn't fair to yourself or anyone else to control your feelings so unnaturally, even if it's anger. How else will anyone know what you feel?

At the same time, if you have angered someone, you must be willing to let them show it. They may need to vent their feelings. They may even need to say bad things about you. They may laugh at you. They may even be justified in feeling that way.

I celebrate freedom with the supper club about eight weeks after prison. Wonderful friends.

You'll survive, words can't kill you. Besides, you can't stop it. Eventually they will tire and those emotions will be spent. Then they will pay closer attention to you, not before.

Constructive anger can be healing. It is truthful. Anger allows us to be honest with ourselves. It is an emotion that we may have to go through, just to get to the other side.

Laughter is the best. It is salve for your wounds, a gift from the gods. How can we live without it? If you can laugh just a little, even at yourself, there is hope for you. People like laughter. It makes you fun and friendly. There is an old Irish saying, "There are three things that are real—God, human folly, and laughter. Since the first two are beyond our comprehension, we must do what we can with the third."

Try to do your best. Sometimes you do. But most times, if you are like me, you do what is necessary to get by. Big mistake. When you fall down hard is when you must try the hardest to do your best. People will be watching you closely. They won't care so much whether you succeed, but they will care mightily if you don't try to do your best. That's all they ask—that you try.

Give and accept unconditional love. I have written several times about my having received unconditional love. I remember one afternoon in Duke Hospital, I received a letter from a young woman who'd once taught Senior High Sunday School with me. She wrote that she didn't know everything that had happened to me or that I'd done, she just wanted me to know that she "was on my side unconditionally." I have never forgotten that person or those thoughts.

It's a good thing that most of us can receive unconditional love. If that weren't so, some of us would never get any love at all. Think about that. When you are the most unlovable is probably when you need it the most, and if there is someone in your life who cares about you that way, hang on to them. And it wouldn't be a bad idea if you were that way yourself toward someone in return.

Learn what makes you happy and do it. I never thought I would be happy waiting tables at my age. I didn't go to college or law school to learn how to be a waiter. Yet more people told me I looked better during that time than at any other time in my life. I learned not to care too much what other people thought. That was a real victory for me. So long as I was happy, and doing something worthwhile, that was enough for me. It should be for you as well.

I remember a former law partner of mine who was making a lot of money practicing law. He told me one day that what he really wanted to do was teach fourth grade. He never will, and there are a lot of fourth grade students who will miss him. And he them.

Learn to forgive yourself and others. It has taken me a long time to forgive myself for all the trouble I caused. I probably am still working on that. Forgiveness is a process. It doesn't have a period to it. You can't control the forgiveness of others toward you, but you can forgive others yourself. It is the most timesaving decision you can make in your recovery, because only when forgiveness takes hold can you go on with your life. Once you've forgiven yourself, you'll never look back.

Go the extra mile. I got really tired of hearing that I had to go the extra mile . . . after mile . . . after mile. I didn't want to hear about the Sermon on the Mount any more. I didn't want to do more than anyone else. I didn't want to hold my head up and be strong. I didn't want to take my lawyers' advice to that effect. I wanted to tell people to shove it. Finally I learned the truth about going that extra mile: it's the right thing to do.

It goes against human nature to go the second or third mile when you really didn't want to go the first one. But it is a necessary part of surrendering yourself to a higher purpose, that of being the best you can be, and this is critical to surviving extreme adversity.

I never, never, never, gave up. Even if I'd stayed in prison longer, I would not have given up.

Always believe in angels. They are all around you. My angels include the gentleman at the Char Grill restaurant, who told me the day before I went to prison that my family could call him any time for help; he was in the phone book. I had never seen him before in my life.

The good friend from Indian Princesses group at the YMCA, who put forty dollars cash in my mailbox at Christmas with a note that read "How-How."

The artist at the Sign of the Fish bookstore who inscribed my name on the front of the Bible I'd received for Christmas from my family. He came out to the front of the store to give it to me personally. He hugged me and told me he was "praying for me."

My fifth-grade teacher, who sent me a check for one hundred dollars and wrote me a letter reminding me of my class trip to Washington, D.C.

The people who came to see me. The ones who called and wrote letters and sent food. The ones who prayed and hoped and became or remained my friends.

Angels are out there. They were there for me. They are there for you as well. Even though you may not always see them, they will lead you home.